PYTHON MASTERY: FROM ABSOLUTE BEGINNER TO PRO

NIBEDITA SAHU

While every precaution has been taken in the preparation of this book, the publisher assumes no responsibility for errors or omissions, or for damages resulting from the use of the information contained herein.

Python Mastery: From Absolute Beginner to Pro

by **Nibedita Sahu**

WRITTEN BY NIBEDITA SAHU

Table of Contents

16. Debugging and Testing: [[316]]

- Debugging techniques and tools (pdb) [[317]]
- Unit testing (unittest module) [[322]]

17. Performance Optimization: [[328]]

- Profiling and optimizing code
  (timeit, cProfile) [[329]]

18. Virtual Environments and Package Management: [[336]]

- Creating and managing virtual environments
  (venv, conda) [[337]]
- Installing and managing packages (pip) [[343]]

19. Python Best Practices: [[348]]

- Code organization and style (PEP 8) [[349]]
- Documentation (docstrings) [[357]]
- Code versioning and collaboration
  (Git, GitHub) [[365]]

Appendix: [[370]]

- Exercises [[371]]
- Solutions [[376]]
- Resources [[384]]
- End-description [[387]]

Preface:

Welcome to "Python Mastery: From Absolute Beginner to Pro"! If you're holding this book, chances are you have an insatiable curiosity for Python programming, a language that has captivated the world of technology and innovation. Whether you're stepping into the exciting world of programming for the first time or seeking to refine your skills, you've come to the right place.

The journey of mastering Python can be both exhilarating and challenging, but fear not – this book is your trusty companion for the road ahead. As a tech enthusiast, author, and Python programmer, I have walked this path myself, and I'm thrilled to share my knowledge and experiences with you.

In these pages, we will embark on an adventure that covers the entire spectrum of Python programming, from its fundamental building blocks to the realm of advanced techniques. Throughout this book, I aim to nurture your understanding, encouraging you to think like a true Python expert rather than memorize lines of code.

Expect to dive into real-world projects, exploring practical applications that will reinforce your learning and ignite your creativity. By the time you reach the final chapter, you will have the confidence to tackle complex coding challenges, develop your projects, and contribute to the vibrant Python community.

Remember, the journey to Python mastery is not just about reaching a destination; it's about the joy of learning and the satisfaction of discovering new possibilities with every line of code you write.

So, without further ado, let's embark on this rewarding journey together. Let's unlock the full potential of Python and embrace the endless opportunities it brings to our fingertips.

Happy coding!

Nibedita Sahu

Description:

Unlock the full potential of Python with this comprehensive and engaging guide that takes you on an exciting journey from an absolute beginner to a seasoned pro! Whether you're a complete novice or already have some programming experience, this book is designed to equip you with the skills and knowledge needed to excel in Python programming.

Why This Book Stands Out:

1. ***Step-by-Step Learning:*** The book follows a structured approach, walking you through Python concepts step by step, making learning smooth and enjoyable.
2. ***Real-World Projects:*** Get hands-on experience by building practical projects that will cement your understanding and prepare you for real coding challenges.
3. ***Mastery, Not Memorization:*** Emphasizing understanding over memorization, this book empowers you to think like a Python expert, enabling you to create your solutions creatively.

What Makes This Book Unique:

1. ***Beyond Basics:*** While it starts from the very basics, this book doesn't stop there. You'll delve into advanced Python topics to sharpen your skills and broaden your horizons.

2. ***In-Depth Coverage:*** From fundamental data types to complex algorithms, ensuring you gain a profound understanding of Python's capabilities.
3. ***Clear Explanations:*** Complex concepts are broken down into simple terms, making even the most intricate topics accessible and easy to comprehend.

<u>Who This Book is For:</u>

1. ***Aspiring Programmers:*** If you're new to programming, this book serves as your friendly guide, introducing you to Python with ease and clarity.
2. ***Intermediate Coders:*** For those familiar with Python basics, this book offers the perfect opportunity to level up your skills and explore advanced techniques.
3. ***Tech Enthusiasts:*** Whether you want to develop web applications, analyze data, or automate tasks, Python is the gateway to a world of possibilities, and this book is your key.

Unlock your programming potential and become a Python pro! Embrace the journey of mastering Python, and let this book be your ultimate companion in this exciting endeavor. The future of coding awaits you; let's embark on this adventure together!

Python Mastery: From Absolute Beginner to Pro

Nibedita Sahu

Chapter 1. Python Mastery (Complete Roadmap)

Python is a versatile and powerful programming language known for its simplicity and readability. From its humble beginnings to becoming one of the most popular languages, Python has gained immense popularity due to its ease of use, extensive libraries, and wide-ranging applications.

This chapter can be somewhat long as I'm covering a wide range of topics. Also, at the end I'll be explaining about what the career opportunities are there, after becoming proficient in Python. So many things to explore yet.

So, have patience, pay attention and finish it.

Let's jump into it right away!

<u>**1.Python Basics**</u>

Python Basics refer to the fundamental concepts and syntax of the Python programming language. It includes topics such as variables, data types, operators, control flow (if statements, loops), functions, modules, input/output, file handling, and exception handling. Understanding these basics is essential for writing and understanding Python code effectively.

a) Variables, data types, and operators:

In Python, variables are used to store data values, and they can hold different data types such as Numbers (integers, floats), Strings, and Booleans. Operators are used to perform operations on variables and data, such as arithmetic (+, -, *, /), comparison (==, <, >), and logical (and, or, not).

b) Control flow (if statements, loops):

Control flow in Python allows you to make decisions and repeat actions based on certain conditions. If statements are used to execute different blocks of code based on whether a condition is true or false. Loops, like the for and while loops, allow you to repeat a block of code multiple times.

c) Functions and modules:

Functions are reusable blocks of code that perform specific tasks. They help organize code and make it more modular. Modules are files that contain Python code, including functions and variables, which can be imported and used in other programs.

d) Input/output and file handling:

Python provides built-in functions to handle input and output operations. These functions allow you to take user input, display output, and work with files. File handling involves opening, reading, writing, and closing files using file objects and specific methods.

e) Exception handling:

Exception handling is a way to handle errors or exceptional conditions that may occur during program execution. By using try-except blocks, you can catch and handle specific exceptions, allowing your program to gracefully handle errors and prevent crashes.

2. Data Structures

Data structures are containers or formats used to organize and store data efficiently. They provide different ways to store, manipulate, and access data elements. Here are the explanations for the specific data structures:

a) Lists, tuples, and dictionaries:

Lists are ordered collections of items, allowing duplicates and mutable operations. Tuples are similar to lists but immutable. Dictionaries are key-value pairs, providing fast lookup based on unique keys.

b) Sets and frozensets:

Sets are unordered collections of unique elements, useful for performing mathematical operations like union, intersection, and difference. Frozensets are immutable sets.

c) Arrays (NumPy):

NumPy is a library in Python that introduces arrays, which are similar to lists but optimized for mathematical operations and handling large datasets efficiently. Arrays provide fast element-wise operations and allow vectorized computations.

d) Series and DataFrames (Pandas):

Pandas is a powerful library for data manipulation and analysis. Series are one-dimensional labeled arrays, while DataFrames are two-dimensional labeled data structures, similar to tables. They offer convenient methods for data cleaning, filtering, and aggregation, making data analysis tasks easier.

3. File Handling

File handling is the way we interact with files in a computer program. It allows us to read information from files, write data to files, and manipulate files in various formats.

a) Reading and writing files:

In Python, we can open a file using the 'open()' function and then read its contents using methods like 'read()' or 'readlines()'. To write to a file, we open it in write mode and use methods like 'write()' or 'writelines()' to add data to the file.

b) CSV and JSON file formats:

CSV (Comma-Separated Values) and JSON (JavaScript Object Notation) are commonly used file formats for storing structured data. CSV files store data in a table-like format with values separated by commas. JSON files store data in a human-readable format using key-value pairs. Python provides convenient libraries such as csv and json to read and write data in these formats, simplifying the handling of CSV and JSON files in Python programs.

4. String Manipulation

String manipulation involves modifying, extracting, and manipulating text in a computer program. It allows you to perform operations on strings such as combining them together, splitting them into smaller parts, finding and replacing specific words or characters, and changing their case.

a) String operations:

String operations in Python provide a wide range of functionalities for working with strings, including concatenation, splitting, searching, replacing, and changing case. These operations give you the flexibility to manipulate strings according to your needs.

b) Regular Operations:

Regular expressions in Python are powerful tools for pattern matching and text manipulation. The re module provides functions to work with regex. Using special characters and symbols, regex allows you to search, extract, or replace specific patterns in strings. For example, re.search() finds the first occurrence, re.findall() extracts all occurrences, and re.sub() replaces matching patterns. To create a regex pattern, use metacharacters like ^, $, *, +, ?, ., etc., along with character classes and groups. Efficiently leveraging regex can simplify complex string operations and enhance data processing tasks.

5. Object-Oriented Programming (OOP)

Object-Oriented Programming (OOP) is a programming paradigm that organizes code into objects, which are instances of classes. It focuses on modeling real-world entities as objects that have attributes (data) and behaviors (methods).

a) Classes and objects:

In OOP, a class is a blueprint or template that defines the structure and behavior of objects. It encapsulates data and methods. An object, in a different way, is an instance of a class. It represents a specific entity with its own unique state and behavior.

b) Inheritance and polymorphism:

Inheritance allows a class to inherit properties and methods from another class, known as the superclass or base class. It promotes code reusability and enables the creation of specialized classes called subclasses or derived classes.

Polymorphism refers to the ability of objects of different classes to be treated as objects of a common superclass. It allows methods to be overridden in subclasses, providing different implementations while maintaining a consistent interface.

c) Advanced OOP concepts:

Advanced OOP concepts include abstraction, encapsulation, and interfaces. Abstraction focuses on hiding unnecessary details and exposing only essential information. Encapsulation involves bundling data and related methods into a single unit, preventing direct access to the internal state of an object. Interfaces define a contract that classes must adhere to, specifying the methods they should implement, promoting loose coupling and modularity in code design.

6. Modules and Packages

Modules and Packages are essential components of modular programming in many programming languages, including Python. They provide a way to organize and reuse code by dividing it into separate files and directories.

a) Creating and importing modules:

In Python, a module is a file containing Python definitions, functions, and statements. You can create your own modules by writing code in a separate .py file. To use a module in another Python script, you import it using the 'import' statement, which allows you to access its functions, variables, and classes.

b) Working with packages:

A package is a way to organize related modules into directories. It helps manage large projects by grouping related functionality together. A package is simply a directory containing a special file called '__init__.py'. To use a module from a package, you specify the package name followed by the module name using dot notation in the import statement.

For example, if you have a package called "my_package" with a module called "my_module", you would import it as follows:

```
import my_package.my_module
```

You can then access the functions or classes from the module using dot notation:

```
my_package.my_module.my_function()
# Change according to your package and module.
```

Overall, modules and packages provide a way to organize code, improve code reusability, and make the development process more efficient and manageable.

7. Error Handling and Exceptions

Error Handling and Exceptions are mechanisms in programming that allow for the detection and management of errors or unexpected events that may occur during the execution of a program.

a) Handling errors and exceptions:

Error handling involves anticipating potential errors and implementing strategies to handle them gracefully, preventing program crashes or undesired behavior. It includes techniques like try-except blocks, where specific code segments are wrapped in a try block and potential errors are caught and handled in except blocks.

b) Try-except blocks:

Try-except blocks are used to catch and handle exceptions. The code within the try block is executed, and if an exception occurs, it is caught by an except block that matches the specific exception type. This allows for controlled error handling, such as displaying an error message, logging the exception, or taking alternative actions to recover from the error and keep the program running smoothly.

8. Functional Programming

Functional Programming is a programming paradigm that emphasizes the use of pure functions, where the output is solely determined by the input and has no side effects. It focuses on treating computation as the evaluation of mathematical functions and promotes immutability and higher-order functions.

a) Lambda functions:

Lambda functions, also known as anonymous functions, are functions without a name. They are defined inline and typically used when a function is required for a short and simple operation. Lambda functions are concise and can be passed as arguments to other functions.

b) Map, filter, and reduce functions:

Map, filter, and reduce are higher-order functions commonly used in functional programming. The map function applies a given function to each element of an iterable and returns a new iterable with the transformed values. The filter function selects elements from an iterable based on a given condition. The reduce function applies a binary function to the elements of an iterable, reducing them to a single value by iteratively combining the elements.

These functions facilitate a functional programming style by allowing operations to be expressed concisely and elegantly, promoting code readability and maintainability.

9. Iterators and Generators

Iterators and Generators are features in Python that enable efficient and controlled iteration over a sequence of elements.

a) Iteration protocols:

Iteration protocols define the set of methods that an object needs to implement in order to be considered an iterator. The two essential methods are '__iter__', which returns the iterator object itself, and '__next__', which retrieves the next element in the sequence. By following these protocols, objects can be iterated using a for loop or by explicitly calling the 'next()' function.

```python
class MyIterator:
    def __iter__(self):
        return self

    def __next__(self):
```

```python
        # Implementation to retrieve the next element
        # ...

my_iter = MyIterator()
for item in my_iter:
    print(item)



"""
If you will pass it
'def __next__(self):
    pass

then your system will throw None coninuosly
 and your sytem can be crashed too. Don't do that 😈
"""
```

b) Creating and using generators:

Generators are a type of iterator that can be created using a special syntax with the 'yield' keyword. They allow you to define a function that behaves like an iterator, generating values on-the-fly without storing them all in memory. Generators are useful when dealing with large or infinite sequences.

```python
def my_generator():
    yield 1
    yield 2
    yield 3
```

```
gen = my_generator()
for item in gen:
    print(item)

# Output
1
2
3
```

The 'my_generator' function is defined with 'yield' statements, and each time the function is called, it returns the next yielded value. This allows for lazy evaluation and memory-efficient iteration.

10. Decorators

Decorators in Python are a way to modify or enhance the behavior of functions or classes without directly modifying their source code.

a) Function decorators:

Function decorators are functions that take another function as input and return a modified version of it. They provide a convenient way to add additional functionality to functions, such as logging, timing, or input validation, by wrapping the original function with additional code.

```python
def decorator(func):
    def wrapper():
        # Additional code before calling the original function
        result = func()
        # Additional code after calling the original function
        return result
    return wrapper


@decorator
def my_function():
    # Original function code
    return result
```

The 'decorator' function takes 'my_function' as input and returns a modified version of it called 'wrapper'. The '@decorator' syntax is a shorthand way to apply the decorator to 'my_function'.

b) Class decorators:

Class decorators work similarly to function decorators but operate on classes instead of functions. They can be used to modify the behavior or attributes of a class.

Class decorators are applied using the '@decorator' syntax above the class definition.

```python
def decorator(cls):
    # Modify the class attributes or behavior
    return cls

@decorator
class MyClass:
    # Class definition
    pass
```

The 'decorator' function takes 'MyClass' as input and returns the modified version of the class itself. The decorator can add or modify attributes, override methods, or perform any other desired modifications to the class.

11. *Working with Dates and Times*

Working with Dates and Times involves manipulating and managing date and time values in programming. In Python, the 'datetime' module provides classes and methods to handle dates, times, and durations.

Date and time manipulation using the 'datetime' module:

The 'datetime' module provides classes such as 'datetime', 'date', 'time', and 'timedelta' to work with dates, times, and durations. These classes offer methods to perform various operations like creating date or time objects, extracting specific components (year, month, day, hour, etc.), performing arithmetic operations, and formatting dates and times.

```python
from datetime import datetime, timedelta

# Creating a datetime object
now = datetime.now()
print(now)   # Output: 2023-05-28 15:57:24.404291

# Accessing date and time components
year = now.year
month = now.month
day = now.day
hour = now.hour
minute = now.minute
second = now.second

# Performing arithmetic operations
future_date = now + timedelta(days=7)
elapsed_time = future_date - now

# Formatting dates and times
formatted_date = now.strftime("%Y-%m-%d")
formatted_time = now.strftime("%H:%M:%S")
```

```
print(formatted_date)  # Output: 2023-05-28
print(formatted_time)  # Output; 15:57:24
```

The 'datetime.now()' function returns the current date and time. We can access specific components using attributes like 'year', 'month', etc. Arithmetic operations like adding or subtracting durations are possible using 'timedelta'. Formatting dates and times is done using the 'strftime' method with format codes to define the desired output format.

12. Python Standard Library

The Python Standard Library is a collection of modules and packages that come bundled with Python. It provides a wide range of functionality, including file operations, system interactions, mathematical calculations, random number generation, and much more.

Exploring commonly used modules (os, sys, math, random, etc.)

a) os:

The 'os' module provides functions for interacting with the operating system. It allows you to perform operations like file and directory management, environment variables access, process management, and more.

```python
import os

# Get the current working directory
current_dir = os.getcwd()

# Create a new directory
os.mkdir('new_directory')

# Rename a file
os.rename('old_file.txt', 'new_file.txt')

# Execute a system command
os.system('ls')
```

b) sys:

The 'sys' module provides access to system-specific parameters and functions. It allows you to interact with the Python runtime environment, access command-line arguments, and manipulate the interpreter's behavior.

```python
import sys

# Get command-line arguments
arguments = sys.argv

# Terminate the program
sys.exit()
```

```python
# Get the version of Python
version = sys.version
```

c) math:

The 'math' module provides mathematical functions and constants. It includes functions for trigonometry, logarithms, exponentiation, rounding, and more.

```python
import math

# Calculate the square root
sqrt = math.sqrt(25)

# Calculate the sine of an angle
sine = math.sin(math.pi/2)

# Calculate the logarithm
logarithm = math.log(10, 2)
```

d) random:

The 'random' module allows for generating random numbers and making random choices. It provides functions for random number generation, shuffling sequences, and selecting random elements.

```python
import random

# Generate a random integer
random_number = random.randint(1, 10)
```

```python
# Shuffle a list
my_list = [1, 2, 3, 4, 5]
random.shuffle(my_list)

# Choose a random element from a
sequence
random_element = random.choice(my_list)
```

These are just a few examples of the modules available in the Python Standard Library. The library offers numerous modules catering to various needs, making Python a powerful and versatile programming language.

13. Working with Databases

Working with databases involves interacting with structured data storage systems, enabling the storage, retrieval, and manipulation of data. In Python, this is achieved through modules that provide database connectivity and SQL (Structured Query Language) support.

a) SQL (SQLite):

SQL is a standard language for managing relational databases. SQLite is a popular and lightweight database engine that supports SQL syntax. It allows you to create and manage databases, define tables, perform CRUD (Create, Read, Update, Delete) operations, and execute complex queries.

b) Database connectivity (SQLite3):

The 'sqlite3' module in Python provides a simple and intuitive API for working with SQLite databases. It allows you to establish connections, create cursor objects to execute SQL statements, and retrieve data from the database. It also supports transactions for atomic operations.

Working with databases can involve more complex operations like joins, indexing, and transactions. However, the 'sqlite3' module provides a solid foundation for working with SQLite databases in Python.

14. Regular Expressions

Regular Expressions (regex) are powerful tools for pattern matching and text manipulation. They provide a concise and flexible syntax for searching, extracting, and manipulating text based on specific patterns. In Python, the 're' module is used to work with regular expressions.

Pattern matching and text manipulation (re module):

The 're' module in Python allows you to work with regular expressions. It provides functions like 'match()', 'search()', 'findall()', and 'sub()' to perform various operations on strings using regex patterns. These functions enable pattern matching, extracting specific text, replacing text, and more.

```python
import re

# Match a pattern at the beginning of a string
result = re.match(r'Hello', 'Hello, World!')
print(result)  # <re.Match object; span=(0, 5), match='Hello'>

# Search for a pattern in a string
result = re.search(r'World', 'Hello, World!')
print(result)  # <re.Match object; span=(7, 12), match='World'>

# Find all occurrences of a pattern in a string
result = re.findall(r'\d+', 'I have 5 apples and 3 oranges')
print(result)  # ['5', '3']

# Substitute a pattern with replacement text
result = re.sub(r'apple', 'banana', 'I have an apple')
print(result)  # I have an banana
```

We use the 're' module to match a pattern at the beginning of a string, search for a pattern in a string, find all occurrences of a pattern, and substitute a pattern with replacement text.

Regular expressions provide a flexible and efficient way to handle complex text processing tasks, allowing you to leverage the power of pattern matching for various purposes like data validation, parsing, and text manipulation.

15. Debugging and Testing

Debugging and testing are crucial aspects of software development that help identify and resolve issues in code and ensure the correctness and reliability of the software.

a) Debugging techniques and tools (pdb):

Debugging is the process of finding and fixing errors or bugs in code. Python provides the 'pdb' module, which is a built-in debugger. It allows you to set breakpoints, step through code execution, inspect variables, and analyze program flow to identify and fix issues.

```python
import pdb

def my_function():
    x = 5
    y = 2
    result = x / (y - 2)
    return result

pdb.set_trace()
result = my_function()
print(result)
```

Setting 'pdb.set_trace()' creates a breakpoint at that line. When the program runs, it pauses at the breakpoint, allowing you to interactively inspect variables, execute code step by step, and diagnose problems.

b) Unit testing (unittest module):

Unit testing is a method of testing individual units or components of software to ensure they function correctly. The 'unittest' module in Python provides a framework for writing and executing unit tests. It allows you to define test cases, test functions, and assertions to verify expected outcomes.

```python
import unittest

def add_numbers(x, y):
    return x + y

class MyTest(unittest.TestCase):
    def test_addition(self):
        result = add_numbers(3, 4)
        self.assertEqual(result, 7)

if __name__ == '__main__':
    unittest.main()
```

A test case class is defined with a test function that checks if the 'add_numbers' function returns the expected result using the 'self.assertEqual()' assertion. Running the script executes the tests and reports the results.

By using debugging techniques and writing comprehensive unit tests, developers can identify and fix issues during development and ensure the reliability and correctness of their code.

16. Performance Optimization

Performance optimization refers to the process of improving the efficiency and speed of a program or system. It involves identifying bottlenecks and implementing changes to enhance its performance.

Profiling and optimizing code (timeit, cProfile)!

a) timeit:

The timeit module in Python is used to measure the execution time of small code snippets. It helps in benchmarking different approaches and comparing their performance.

b) cProfile:

cProfile is a Python module used for profiling code, which means analyzing the execution time of different functions and identifying areas that consume the most resources. It provides detailed information about the time taken by each function, helping developers optimize their code by focusing on the critical sections.

Both timeit and cProfile are valuable tools in performance optimization as they help developers understand where their code is spending the most time and resources, enabling them to make informed decisions on how to improve its efficiency.

17. Virtual Environments and Package Management

Virtual environments and package management are crucial aspects of software development and deployment.

Virtual environments provide isolated environments for Python projects, allowing developers to have separate Python installations and packages for different projects. This helps avoid conflicts between dependencies and ensures project-specific requirements are met.

a) Creating and managing virtual environments:

Python provides built-in modules like 'venv' and external tools like 'conda' for creating and managing virtual environments. These tools allow developers to set up isolated environments with specific Python versions and packages, enabling them to work on different projects without interference.

b) Installing and managing packages:

Package management tools like pip are used to install, upgrade, and manage external packages and dependencies within a virtual environment. Pip simplifies the process of adding new packages to a project, ensuring the required libraries are readily available for use.

By using virtual environments and package management tools, developers can maintain clean and organized project structures, easily manage dependencies, and ensure consistent and reproducible environments for their Python projects.

18. Python Best Practices

Python best practices refer to the recommended guidelines and approaches for writing clean, efficient, and maintainable Python code.

a) Code organization and style:

Following the guidelines outlined in PEP 8 (Python Enhancement Proposal) helps ensure consistent code organization and style. It covers aspects such as indentation, naming conventions, line length, and code structure, making the code more readable and easier to understand for other developers.

b) Documentation:

Including docstrings in functions, classes, and modules is essential for documenting the purpose, usage, and parameters of the code. Docstrings serve as self-contained documentation and provide valuable information for developers who might need to use or modify the code in the future.

c) Code versioning and collaboration:

Utilizing version control systems like Git and collaboration platforms like GitHub facilitates efficient code management and collaboration among developers. Version control allows tracking changes, branching, and merging, while platforms like GitHub provide a centralized location for hosting code repositories, managing issues, and facilitating collaboration through features like pull requests.

By adhering to these Python best practices, developers can enhance code readability, maintainability, and collaboration, leading to more efficient development workflows and improved code quality.

After mastering Python, you open the door to a wide range of exciting and rewarding career opportunities. Here are some of the paths you can pursue:

- ***Software Developer/Engineer:***

Python is extensively used in software development, making it a valuable skill for becoming a professional software developer or engineer. You can contribute to building robust applications, web development, data analysis, scientific computing, and much more.

- ***Data Scientist:***

Python's extensive libraries, such as NumPy, Pandas, and scikit-learn, make it a top choice for data science and analysis.

With Python mastery, you can work with large datasets, perform complex data manipulation, develop machine learning models, and gain insights from data to drive business decisions.

- ***Machine Learning Engineer:***

Python is widely used in the field of machine learning and artificial intelligence.

Mastering Python allows you to work with popular frameworks like TensorFlow and PyTorch, enabling you to develop and deploy machine learning models for various applications.

- ***Data Engineer:***

Python's versatility extends to data engineering tasks, including data extraction, transformation, and loading (ETL). With Python, you can automate data workflows, build scalable data pipelines, and work with big data technologies like Apache Spark.

- ***DevOps Engineer:***

Python's simplicity and vast ecosystem make it an excellent choice for automating deployment, configuration management, and infrastructure orchestration. With Python expertise, you can pursue a career in DevOps, ensuring smooth and efficient software delivery and infrastructure management.

- ***Web Developer:***

Python's web frameworks like Django and Flask empower developers to create dynamic, scalable, and secure web applications. Mastery of Python equips you with the skills to develop backend logic, handle databases, and build robust web APIs.

- ***Cybersecurity Professional:***

Python is commonly used for various cybersecurity tasks, such as penetration testing, vulnerability assessment, and security automation.

With Python proficiency, you can contribute to strengthening the security of systems and networks.

- ***Freelancer/Consultant:***

Python's popularity and versatility make it an in-demand skill for freelancers and consultants. You can offer your expertise in Python development, data analysis, automation, or specialized domains to clients across industries.

Mastering Python opens up a vast array of career opportunities across industries like technology, finance, healthcare, e-commerce, and more. The versatility and wide adoption of Python ensure that your skills remain valuable and in high demand in the ever-evolving world of technology.

Happy Pythoning! 😊

Chapter 2. Python Basics

2.1. VARIABLES AND DATA TYPES

Python is a versatile and powerful programming language that is widely used in various domains, such as web development, data analysis, machine learning, and more. One of the fundamental concepts in Python programming is variables and types. Variables allow us to store and manipulate data, while types define the nature of the data and how it can be operated upon.

In Python, variables serve as containers for storing values. They can hold different types of data, including numbers, strings, lists, dictionaries, and more. The flexibility of variables in Python allows for dynamic typing, meaning that variables can change their type as needed during runtime. This makes Python a highly flexible and adaptable language for various programming tasks.

To understand variables and types in Python, let's start by exploring the different data types available in the language.

1. Numeric Types:

Python provides several numeric types to represent numbers. The most commonly used numeric types are integers ("int") and floating-point numbers ("float"). Integers are whole numbers without decimal points, while floating-point numbers can have decimal places.

```
# Numeric Types
x = 5         # assigning an integer value to x
y = 3.14      # assigning a floating-point value to y


print(x)      # Output: 5
print(y)      # Output: 3.14
print(x+y)    # Output: 8.14
```

2. *Strings:*

Strings are used to represent textual data in Python. They are enclosed in single quotes (') or double quotes ("). Strings are immutable, meaning that once defined, their values cannot be changed. However, new strings can be created by manipulating existing ones.

```
# Strings
name = "Nibedita Sahu"    # assigning a string value to name
message = 'Hello, ' + name + '!'   # concatenating strings


print(name)       # Output: Nibedita Sahu
print(message)    # Output: Hello, Nibedita Sahu!
```

3. *Lists:*

Lists are a versatile data type in Python that can hold a collection of values. They are ordered and mutable, which means that elements can be added, removed, or modified.

Lists are defined by enclosing comma-separated values in square brackets ('[]').

```python
# Lists
numbers = [1, 2, 3, 4, 5]   # defining a list of numbers
fruits = ['apple', 'banana', 'orange']   # defining a list of strings

mixed = [1, 'apple', 3.14, True]   # a list with mixed data types

print(numbers)   # Output: [1, 2, 3, 4, 5]
print(fruits)        # Output: ['apple', 'banana', 'orange']
print(mixed)        # Output: [1, 'apple', 3.14, True]

print(fruits + numbers)
# Output: ['apple', 'banana', 'orange', 1, 2, 3, 4, 5]
```

4. Tuples:

Tuples are similar to lists, but they are immutable, meaning their elements cannot be modified after creation. Tuples are defined by enclosing comma-separated values in parentheses ('()').

```python
# Tuples
point = (3, 4)   # defining a tuple representing a 2D point
person = ('Nibe', 20, 'nibe@example.com')   # defining a tuple representing a person's information

print(person)
# Output: ('Nibe', 20, 'nibe@example.com')
```

```
print(point)          # Output: (3, 4)
print(point+person)
# Output: (3, 4, 'Nibe', 20, 'nibe@example.com')
```

5. Dictionaries:

Dictionaries are used to store key-value pairs. Each value is associated with a unique key, which can be used to access the corresponding value. Dictionaries are defined by enclosing key-value pairs in curly braces ('{}').

```
# Dictionaries
student = {'name': 'Nibedita Sahu', 'age': 20, 'grade': 'A'}
# defining a dictionary representing a student

print(student)
# Output: {'name': 'Nibedita Sahu', 'age': 20, 'grade': 'A'}
```

Now that we have explored the various data types in Python let's delve into variables and their usage.

In Python, variables are created by assigning a value to a name using the assignment operator ('='). Variable names can contain letters, digits, and underscores but cannot start with a digit. They are case-sensitive, meaning that 'var' and 'var' are treated as different variables.

```
# Variables
x = 7  # assigning the value 7to the variable x
```

```python
message = "Hello, World!"
# assigning a string to the variable message

print(x)            # Output: 7
print(message)          # Output: Hello, World!

# Another fun
print(x + message)
# TypeError: unsupported operand type(s) for +: 'int' and
'str'

print(str(x) + message)     # Output: 7Hello, World!
```

Variables can be used in expressions to perform operations and store the results. They can also be reassigned to new values. Here's an example showcasing the usage of variables:

```python
# Variable usage
radius = 5
pi = 3.14
print(radius)           # Output: 5

# Calculating the area of a circle
area = pi * (radius ** 2)
print(area)             # Output: 78.5

# Updating the value of radius
radius = 7
print(radius)           # Output: 7
```

```python
# Calculating the new area of the circle
new_area = pi * (radius ** 2)
print(new_area)        # Output: 153.86
```

In the above code snippet, we first assign the value 5 to the variable 'radius' and 3.14 to the variable 'pi'. Then, we calculate the area of a circle using the formula 'pi * radius^2' and store the result in the variable 'area'. Next, we update the value of 'radius' to 7 and calculate the new area based on the updated radius, storing it in the variable 'new_area'.

Variables can also be used to store the results of functions or expressions. For example, we can use variables to store the output of a mathematical calculation, the length of a string, or the result of a conditional operation.

```python
# Variable usage with functions
sentence = "The quick brown fox jumps over the lazy dog."
sentence_length = len(sentence)   # storing the length of
the string in a variable

print(sentence_length)      # Output: 44

is_long_sentence = sentence_length > 50   # storing the
result of a comparison in a variable
print(is_long_sentence)      # Output: False
```

In the code snippet above, we calculate the length of the string 'sentence' using the 'len()' function and store the result in the variable 'sentence_length'. We then store the result of a comparison (sentence_lenght>50) in the variable 'is_long_sentence'. This allows us to reuse these values later in the program or manipulate them further.

Python provides several built-in functions that can be used to convert variables from one type to another. These functions are useful when we need to perform operations or comparisons between variables of different types. Here are some commonly used types conversion functions:

- int(): Converts a variable to an integer type.
- float(): Converts a variable to a floating-point type.
- str(): Converts a variable to a string type.
- list(): Converts a variable to a list type.
- tuple(): Converts a variable to a tuple type.
- dict(): Converts a variable to a dictionary type.

Let's look at an example to understand how type conversion works:

```python
# Type conversion
x = 5
y = "10"
print(x+y)
# TypeError: unsupported operand type(s) for +: 'int' and 'str'
```

```python
z = float(x) + int(y)
# converting x to float and y to int, then performing addition

print(z)   # Output: 15.0

#You can also try different things of your own and have fun:)
```

In the above code snippet, we have an integer variable 'x' with a value of 5 and a string variable 'y' with a value of "10". To perform addition, we convert 'x' to a float using the 'float()' function and 'y' to an int using the 'int()' function. After conversion, we add the two variables and store the result in the variable 'z'. Finally, we print the value of 'z', which is 15.0.

Python supports dynamic typing, which means that we can change the type of a variable by assigning a value of a different type to it. This flexibility allows us to write concise and flexible code. However, it's important to handle type conversions carefully to avoid unexpected results or errors.

In addition to the basic data types, we discussed earlier, Python provides several specialized data types and modules that extend its functionality. Some notable ones include:

6. Sets:

Sets are used to store a collection of unique elements. They are defined by enclosing comma-separated values in curly braces ('{}'). Sets are useful for tasks such as removing duplicates from a list or checking membership efficiently.

```python
# Sets
fruits = {"apple", "banana", "orange"}
fruits.add("mango")   # adding an element to the set
print(fruits)
# Output: {'apple', 'mango', 'orange', 'banana'}
```

7. Booleans:

Booleans represent the truth values True and False. They are often used in conditional statements and control flow. Comparisons and logical operations yield Boolean values.

```python
# Booleans
is_raining = True
is_sunny = False

if is_raining:
    print("Take an umbrella.")
else:
    print("That's alright!")

if not is_sunny:
    print("Wear a jacket.")
else:
    print("Follow your fashion!")
```

```python
# Output:
# Take an umbrella.
# Wear a jacket.

# Also try yourself by modifying the code! 
```

8. *Modules:*

Python provides a vast collection of modules that offer additional functionality beyond the built-in types. Modules are libraries of code that can be imported and used in your Python programs. Some popular modules include 'math' for mathematical operations, 'random' for random number generation, and 'datetime' for working with dates and times.

```python
# Modules
import math

radius = 5
circumference = 2 * math.pi * radius
# using the math module to calculate the circumference

print(circumference)   # Output: 31.41592653589793
```

Understanding variables and types is fundamental to Python programming. Variables allow us to store and manipulate data, while types define the nature of the data and how it can be operated upon. Python offers a wide range of data types, from numeric types and strings to lists, dictionaries, and more.

By effectively using variables and understanding their types, you can write robust, flexible, and efficient Python programs. You can perform operations, comparisons, and manipulations on variables based on their types, and Python's dynamic typing allows for flexibility in handling different data types.

Furthermore, Python provides various built-in functions for type conversion, allowing you to convert variables from one type to another when necessary. This feature is particularly useful when dealing with user input or performing calculations involving different data types.

Python's versatility extends beyond the basic data types we discussed. Specialized data types, such as Sets, Booleans, and Modules, offer additional functionality and cater to specific programming needs. Sets are useful for storing unique elements and performing set operations, booleans are essential for conditional statements and logical operations, while modules provide extensive libraries for various purposes, including mathematics, random number generation, and date/time manipulation.

As you continue your journey in Python programming, it's important to practice using variables effectively and understand how different data types can be used to your advantage. Here are some tips to keep in mind:

- ***Choose meaningful variable names:*** Select names that reflect the purpose and meaning of the data stored in the variable. This improves code readability and makes it easier for others (or your future self) to understand your code.

- ***Be mindful of variable scope:*** Variables have different scopes, such as local and global. Understanding scope is crucial to avoid naming conflicts and ensure that variables are accessible where needed.

- ***Handle type conversions carefully:*** When converting variables from one type to another, be aware of potential data loss or unexpected results. Ensure that the conversion is appropriate for the intended operation and validate user input when necessary.

- ***Utilize Python's rich library ecosystem:*** Python's strength lies in its extensive library ecosystem. Explore and utilize libraries to leverage existing solutions and streamline your programming tasks. Remember to import the required modules and familiarize yourself with their documentation.

- ***Test and debug your code:*** Always test your code with different scenarios and inputs to ensure its correctness and reliability. Debugging tools and techniques are invaluable for identifying and resolving issues in your code.

By mastering variables and types in Python, you gain a solid foundation for building more complex programs and exploring advanced concepts, such as object-oriented programming, data analysis, or machine learning.

In summary, variables and types form the backbone of Python programming. They allow you to store, manipulate, and operate on data efficiently. Understanding the different data types available, practicing effective variable usage, and being aware of type conversions will empower you to write elegant and functional Python code. Embrace the power of variables and types in Python and let your programming journey flourish!

2.2. OPERATORS

Python is a versatile and powerful programming language that offers a wide range of operators to perform various operations on data. In this section, we will delve into the world of operators in Python, exploring their types, functions, and how they can be used to manipulate and process data efficiently.

1. Arithmetic Operators:

Arithmetic operators are used to perform mathematical calculations such as addition, subtraction, multiplication, division, modulus, and exponentiation.

```python
# Addition
result = 5 + 3
print(result)       # Output: 8

# Subtraction
result = 10 - 4
print(result)       # Output: 6

# Multiplication
result = 2 * 3
print(result)       # Output: 6

# Division
result = 15 / 4
print(result)       # Output: 3.75
```

```
# Modulus (Remainder)
result = 15 % 4
print(result)      # Output: 3

# Exponentiation
result = 2 ** 4
print(result)       # Output: 16
```

2. *Assignment Operators:*

Assignment operators are used to assign values to variables.
They provide a convenient way to update and modify
variables based on their previous values.

```
# Simple Assignment
x = 10

# Addition Assignment
x += 5              # Equivalent to: x = x + 5

# Subtraction Assignment
x -= 3              # Equivalent to: x = x - 3

# Multiplication Assignment
x *= 2              # Equivalent to: x = x * 2

# Division Assignment
x /= 4              # Equivalent to: x = x / 4
```

3. _Comparison Operators:_

Comparison operators are used to compare values and return a Boolean result (True or False). These operators are handy when it comes to making decisions or performing conditional operations.

```python
# Equal to
result = 5 == 5
print(result)      # Output: True


# Not equal to
result = 5 != 5
print(result)      # Output: False


# Greater than
result = 10 > 5
print(result)      # Output: True


# Less than or equal to
result = 3 <= 2
print(result)      # Output: False
```

Or with another way, you can write your code like this as well. First define two variables and then just compare them one by one or at once.

```python
#COMPARISON OPERATORS
n = 10
s = 7
print(n>s)      # Output: True
print(n>=s)      # Output: True
```

```
print(n<s)      # Output: False
print(n<=s)     # Outp[ut: False
print(n==s)     # Output: False
print(n!=s)     # Output: True

# Or you can write in one line!
print(n>5, n<5, n==5, n!=s)
# Output: True False False True
```

4. Logical Operators:

Logical operators allow us to combine multiple conditions and perform logical operations such as AND, OR, and NOT. They are widely used in decision-making and control flow statements.

```
# AND Operator
result = True and False
print(result)         # Output: False

# OR Operator
result = True or False
print(result)         # Output: True

# NOT Operator
result = not True
print(result)         # Output: False
```

5. Membership Operators:

Membership operators are used to test whether a value or variable is present in a sequence, such as a list, tuple, or string. The two membership operators in Python are 'in' and 'not in'.

```python
# in Operator
result = 'a' in 'apple'
print(result)            # Output: True


# not in Operator
result = 'b' not in 'apple'
print(result)            # Output: True
```

6. *Identity Operators:*

Identity operators are used to compare the memory locations of two objects. These operators check if two variables refer to the same object or not. The two identity operators in Python are 'is' and 'is not'.

```python
# is Operator
x = [1, 2, 3]
y = x
result = y is x
print(result)            # Output: True


# is not Operator
x = [1, 2, 3]
y = [1, 2, 3]
result = y is not x
print(result)            # Output: True
```

<u>*7. Bitwise Operators:*</u>

Bitwise operators perform operations on individual bits of binary numbers. These operators are useful in scenarios where you need to manipulate data at a lower level.

```python
# Bitwise AND
result = 5 & 3
print(result)       # Output: 1

# Bitwise OR
result = 5 | 3
print(result)       # Output: 7

# Bitwise XOR
result = 5 ^ 3
print(result)       # Output: 6

# Bitwise NOT
result = ~5
print(result)       # Output: -6

# Bitwise Left Shift
result = 5 << 1
print(result)       # Output: 10

# Bitwise Right Shift
result = 5 >> 1
print(result)       # Output: 2
```

Now let's explore some more things in the Operators world!

- ***<u>Operator Precedence:</u>***

Operator precedence refers to the order in which operators are evaluated in an expression. Python follows specific rules for operator precedence to ensure that expressions are evaluated correctly. It's essential to understand these rules to avoid unexpected results. Like:

- ***Parentheses:*** The expressions within parentheses are evaluated first.
- ***Exponentiation:*** Exponentiation is performed next.
- ***Multiplication, Division, and Modulus:*** These operators are evaluated from left to right.
- ***Addition and Subtraction:*** These operators are evaluated from left to right.
- ***Comparison Operators:*** These operators are evaluated next.
- ***Logical Operators:*** The logical operators 'not', 'and', and 'or' are evaluated in that order.
- ***Assignment Operators:*** The assignment operators are evaluated last.

It's important to note that you can use parentheses to override the default precedence and explicitly specify the order of evaluation in complex expressions.

- ***Operator Overloading:***

In Python, operator overloading allows you to define how operators behave for user-defined objects. This feature gives you the ability to use operators such as '+', '-', ' *', and '==' on your custom classes. By implementing special methods in your classes, you can customize the behavior of operators.

```python
class Vector:
    def __init__(self, x, y):
        self.x = x
        self.y = y

    def __add__(self, other):
        new_x = self.x + other.x
        new_y = self.y + other.y
        return Vector(new_x, new_y)

    def __eq__(self, other):
        return self.x == other.x and self.y == other.y


# Usage
v1 = Vector(1, 2)
v2 = Vector(3, 4)
v3 = v1 + v2
print(v3.x, v3.y)    # Output: 4 6

print(v1 == v2)      # Output: False
```

Here, we defined the '__add__' method to add two 'vector' objects together. We also implemented the '__eq__' method to compare the equality of two 'vector' objects using the '==' operator. This showcases the power of operator overloading in Python.

If you didn't understand this example, then don't worry about that. For now just have a look and try to understand how it works and its uses. We'll explore each and everything with step-by-step. We are going slowly, because understanding is also important. If we will proceed without knowing the basics first then we will be facing problems in future. No need to be worried about anything you are not getting right now. Just take the codes, try yourself, do some changes and get errors. Then you will be getting the ones you were not getting before. 😄

Operators in Python are essential tools for manipulating, comparing, and evaluating data. We explored various types of operators, including arithmetic, assignment, comparison, logical, membership, identity, bitwise, and operator precedence. We also touched upon the concept of operator overloading.

By mastering the usage of operators, you can write concise and expressive code to solve a wide range of problems. It is recommended to practice using operators in different scenarios to become comfortable with their usage.

Remember, operators are like building blocks that allow you to construct complex algorithms and programs. Embrace their power and unleash your creativity in Python programming. Do not hurry! 😄

2.3. Control flow (if statements, loops)

In the world of programming, control flow refers to the order in which statements are executed. It allows us to dictate the flow of our program, making it more dynamic and responsive to different conditions and inputs.

Python, a versatile and popular programming language, offers powerful control flow mechanisms that enable developers to build complex and efficient applications.

In this section, we will dive deep into Python's control flow features, covering conditional statements, loops, and control flow keywords.

1. Conditional Statements

Conditional statements allow us to control the flow of our program based on certain conditions. They help us make decisions and execute different blocks of code depending on whether a condition is true or false.

a) if statement:

The 'if' statement is the simplest form of a conditional statement. It executes a block of code if a specified condition is true.

```python
age = 20
if age >= 18:
    print("You are eligible to vote.")

# Output: You are eligible to vote.
```

Here, 'if' statement checks if the variable 'age' is greater than or equal to 18. If the condition is true, it prints the message "You are eligible to vote." Otherwise, it moves on to the next block of code.

b) else statement:

The 'else' statement allows us to specify a block of code that will be executed if the condition in the 'if' statement is false.

```python
age = 15
if age >= 18:
    print("You are eligible to vote.")
else:
    print("You are not yet eligible to vote.")

# Output: You are not yet eligible to vote.
```

In this case, since the value of 'age' is 15 (is less than 18), the 'if' condition is false, and the code inside the 'else' block is executed. It prints the message "You are not yet eligible to vote."

c) elif statement:

The 'elif' statement is used when we want to test multiple conditions. It stands for "else if" and allows us to chain multiple conditions together.

```python
score = 85
if score >= 90:
    print("Your grade is A.")
elif score >= 80:
    print("Your grade is B.")
elif score >= 70:
    print("Your grade is C.")
else:
    print("Your grade is D.")

# Output: Your grade is B.
```

In this code snippet, the program evaluates the score and prints the corresponding grade based on the conditions. If the score is 85, the 'elif' statement 'score≥80' is true, and it prints "Your grade is B."

2. Loops

Loops are used to repeat a block of code multiple times. They allow us to perform iterative tasks and process data more efficiently.

Python provides two main types of loops: 'for' loops and 'while' loops.

a) for loop:

The 'for' loop iterates over a sequence of elements and executes a block of code for each element.

```python
fruits = ["apple", "banana", "orange"]
for fruit in fruits:
    print(fruit)


# Output
apple
banana
orange


# or if you want it to come in one line with a space-
separated, then:
for fruit in fruits:
    print(fruit, end=" ")


# Output: apple banana orange
# You can modify according to your needs and fun! 😀
```

In this code snippet, the 'for' loop iterates over each element in the 'fruit' list and prints it.

b) while loop:

The 'while' loop continues executing a block of code as long as a specified condition remains true.

```python
count = 0
while count < 5:
    print(count)
    count += 1

# Output:
0
1
2
3
4


"""
Here if you won't increments it by 1 (count += 1), then
it will continuously be throwing 0 0 0 0 0... until you
stop it.
When you will stop running it'll say
"KeyboardInterrupt"
Don't do this, else your system can be crashed too!
"""
```

In this code snippet, the 'while' loop runs until the value of 'count' is less than 5. It prints the value of 'count' and increments it by 1 in each iteration.

3. Control Flow Keywords

Python provides additional control flow keywords that allow us to modify the behavior of loops and conditional statements.

a) break:

The 'break' keyword is used to exit a loop prematurely. When encountered, it immediately terminates the loop and resumes execution at the next statement outside the loop.

```python
numbers = [1, 2, 3, 4, 5]
for number in numbers:
    if number == 3:
        break
    print(number)


# Output:
1
2



# But if you will do something like this:
for number in numbers:
    if number == -3:
        break
```

```
    print(number)

# output:
1
2
3
4
5

# Modify the code & try yourself, get errors and see
how exciting is this!
```

In this code snippet, the loop will terminate when it
encounters the number 3. Take this code, see what it
runs, then do changes of your own, it's okay to get
errors, it's another moment when you solve something
of your own after getting errors. You can modify as per
your needs & fun! 😁

b) continue:

The 'continue' keyword is used to skip the rest of the
code within a loop for the current iteration and move to
the next iteration.

```
numbers = [1, 2, 3, 4, 5]
for number in numbers:
    if number == 3:
        continue
    print(number)
```

```
# output:
1
2
4
5
```

In this code snippet, when the loop reaches the number 3, it skips the 'print' statement and moves on to the next iteration.

c) pass:

The 'pass' keyword is used as a placeholder when a statement is syntactically required but doesn't need to do anything. It acts as a null operation and allows the code to pass through without any action.

```
number = 10
if number > 5:
    pass
else:
    print("Number is less than or equal to 5.")

# Output: It will simply pass the function and won't return anything!
```

In this code snippet, the 'pass' statement is used to indicate that no action is needed when the condition is

true. If the number is less than or equal to 5, it executes
the 'print' statement.

4. _Nesting Control Flow Statements_

One of the powerful aspects of control flow in Python is the
ability to nest control flow statements within each other.

This nesting allows us to create more complex decision-
making and looping structures.

```python
grade = 75
if grade >= 60:
    if grade >= 90:
        print("You achieved an A grade!")
    elif grade >= 80:
        print("You achieved a B grade!")
    else:
        print("You achieved a C grade.")
else:
    print("You did not pass the exam.")

# Output: You achieved a C grade.
```

In this code snippet, we have nested 'if', 'elif', and 'else'
statements inside the outer 'if' statement. Depending on the
value of 'grade', it will execute the corresponding block of
code. This demonstrates the flexibility and expressiveness of
control flow in Python.

5. Control Flow in Real-World Applications

Control flow is a fundamental concept that plays a crucial role in various real-world applications.

Let's explore a few scenarios where control flow is commonly used!

a) User Input Validation:

When developing interactive programs, it is essential to validate user input to ensure it meets specific criteria. Control flow allows us to check the validity of user input and prompt them to enter correct information if necessary.

```python
age = int(input("Enter your age: "))
if age >= 18:
    print("You are eligible to enter.")
else:
    print("You are too young to enter.")


# Input: Enter your age: 20
# Output: You are eligible to enter.


# Input: Enter your age: 14
# Output: You are too young to enter.
```

In this code snippet, the program prompts the user to enter their age. The 'if' statement checks if the age is

greater than or equal to 18 and displays the appropriate
message.

b) *Data Filtering and Processing:*

Control flow is often used in data filtering and processing
tasks. It allows us to iterate over datasets, apply specific
conditions, and perform actions based on the results.

```python
numbers = [1, 2, 3, 4, 5, 6, 7, 8, 9, 10]
even_sum = 0
odd_sum = 0
for number in numbers:
    if number % 2 == 0:
        even_sum += number
    else:
        odd_sum += number
print("Sum of even numbers:", even_sum)
print("Sum of odd numbers:", odd_sum)


# Output:
Sum of even numbers: 30
Sum of odd numbers: 25
```

In this code snippet, the 'for' loop iterates over each
number in the 'numbers' list. The 'if' statement checks if
the number is even or odd and accumulates the sum
accordingly. Finally, it prints the sum of even numbers
and the sum of odd numbers.

c) Program Flow Control:

Control flow keywords like 'break' and 'continue' allow us to control the execution flow within loops. They help us optimize our programs and avoid unnecessary iterations.

- break:

```
names = ["Nibe", "Dita", "Nibedita", "NS"]
for name in names:
    if name == "Nibedita":
        break
    print(name)

# Output:
Nibe
Dita
```

- Continue:

```
names = ["Nibe", "Dita", "Nibedita", "NS"]
for name in names:
    if name == "Nibedita":
        continue
    print(name)

# Output:
Nibe
Dita
NS
```

Control flow is a fundamental concept in programming, and Python provides a rich set of features to handle it effectively. In this article, we explored conditional statements, including 'if', 'else', and 'elif', which allow us to make decisions based on conditions. We also discussed loops, such as 'for' and 'while', which enable us to iterate over sequences and repeat blocks of code.

Additionally, we examined control flow keywords like 'break', 'continue', and 'pass', which provide additional control and flexibility within loops and conditional statements.

With a solid understanding of control flow in Python, you can create dynamic and efficient programs that respond to various conditions and input. So, keep practicing and exploring the possibilities of control flow, and you'll be well-equipped to write robust and adaptable code.

2.4. Functions and Modules

In the realm of programming, efficiency and organization play pivotal roles in the development process. Python, a versatile and popular programming language, provides developers with powerful tools to create clean, readable, and maintainable code. Two essential concepts that aid in achieving these goals are functions and modules. In this section, we will explore functions and modules in Python, their significance, and how they contribute to code modularity, reusability, and overall program structure.

I. Functions: The Building Blocks of Python Programs

Functions in Python are blocks of organized and reusable code that perform specific tasks. They encapsulate a sequence of instructions, allowing us to break down complex problems into smaller, manageable components. By implementing functions, we can enhance code readability, promote code reuse, and improve the overall maintainability of our programs.

1. Defining Functions:

To define a function in Python, we use the 'def' keyword followed by the function name and a pair of parentheses.

```
def add_numbers(a, b):
   return a + b
```

2. Calling Functions:

Once we define a function, we can call it multiple times throughout our program. Calling a function executes the instructions within its block and returns the result, if any. Here's how we call the 'add_numbers' function from earlier:

```
result = add_numbers(5, 7)
print(result)          # Output: 12
```

3. Function Parameters and Arguments:

Functions in Python can accept parameters, which act as placeholders for values that are passed when calling the function. These values are known as arguments. Let's modify our 'add_numbers' function to demonstrate the concept:

```
def add_numbers(a, b):
   return a + b

result = add_numbers(5, 7)
print(result)          # Output: 12
```

4. Default Parameters:

Python functions can also have default parameter values. These values are used when an argument is not provided during the function call. Let's enhance our 'add_numbers' function to include a default parameter:

```python
def add_numbers(a, b=0):
    return a + b

result = add_numbers(5)
print(result)          # Output: 5
```

II. Modules: Organizing Code into Reusable Units

While functions help break down complex problems, modules serve as containers to organize related functions, classes, and variables into reusable units. Modules facilitate code separation, promote code reuse, and allow for better project scalability.

1. Creating Modules:

In Python, a module is simply a file containing Python code. By grouping related functions and classes in a module, we can organize our codebase effectively. Let's create a module called 'math_operations.py':

```python
# math_operations.py

def add_numbers(a, b):
    return a + b

def multiply_numbers(a, b):
    return a * b
```

2. _Importing Modules:_

To use the functions defined in a module, we need to import it into our current script. Python provides multiple ways to import modules:

- ***Importing the entire module:***

```
Importing the entire module:
import math_operations

result = math_operations.add_numbers(5, 7)
print(result)              # Output: 12
```

- ***Importing specific functions:***

```
from math_operations import add_numbers,
multiply_numbers

result = add_numbers(5, 7)
print(result)              # Output: 12
```

- **Importing with an alias:**

```
from math_operations import add_numbers as add

result = add(5, 7)
print(result)              # Output: 12
```

3. Standard Library Modules:

Python also provides a rich set of standard library modules that offer a wide range of functionalities. These modules cover various domains such as mathematics, file handling, network operations, and more. To use these modules, we can import them into our programs.

```python
import random

random_number = random.randint(1, 10)
print(random_number)
```

III. Benefits of Functions and Modules

1. Code Reusability:

Functions and modules promote code reusability, allowing us to use the same code across different parts of a program or even in different projects. Instead of rewriting the same code, we can simply call functions or import modules, saving time and effort.

2. Modularity:

Functions and modules enable us to break down complex problems into smaller, more manageable pieces. This modular approach enhances code readability and makes it easier to understand and maintain.

3. Encapsulation:

Functions encapsulate a sequence of instructions and provide a clear interface for interacting with the code. This encapsulation allows us to hide the internal implementation details and focus on the function's purpose and input/output.

4. Testing and Debugging:

Functions and modules facilitate testing and debugging processes. By isolating specific functionality within functions or modules, we can easily write test cases and pinpoint issues when errors occur.

5. Collaboration:

Functions and modules enhance collaboration among developers. When working in a team, functions and modules provide a standardized way of organizing code. They allow team members to work on different parts of a project independently while ensuring compatibility and code consistency.

IV. Best Practices for Functions and Modules

1. Function Naming:

Choose descriptive and meaningful names for functions that accurately represent their purpose and functionality. Follow

Python's naming conventions, using lowercase letters and underscores to separate words (e.g., 'calculate_average', 'process_data').

2. Function Length and Complexity:

Aim for functions that are concise, focused, and perform a single task. Avoid creating functions that are overly long or perform too many operations. Split complex functions into smaller, reusable functions for better code maintainability.

3. Function Documentation:

Provide clear and concise documentation for your functions, including information about their purpose, parameters, return values, and any side effects. Good documentation helps other developers understand and utilize your functions effectively.

4. Module Structure:

Organize related functions, classes, and variables within a module based on their functionality or purpose. Use comments and docstrings to provide an overview of the module and document important details about the code within.

5. Module Imports:

Import only the necessary functions or classes from a module to avoid cluttering the namespace. If a module contains a large number of functions, importing specific functions can improve code readability and avoid potential naming conflicts.

6. Module Reusability:

When creating modules, strive for high reusability. Ensure that the module can be used in different contexts without tight coupling to specific parts of the program. Create modules with clear boundaries and well-defined interfaces.

In this section, we learned about Functions and Modules.

Functions and modules are fundamental concepts in Python that greatly contribute to code organization, reusability, and maintainability. By utilizing functions, we can break down complex problems into smaller, manageable components, while modules allow us to organize related code into reusable units.

Adhering to best practices such as choosing descriptive names, creating modular and concise functions, and properly documenting code helps improve collaboration, code readability, and ease of maintenance.

Harnessing the power of functions and modules in Python empowers developers to write clean, modular, and efficient code, fostering better software development practices and accelerating the development process. So, embrace functions and modules as your allies in Python programming, and unlock their potential to create elegant and robust solutions.

2.5. Input/Output and File Handling

Python, known for its simplicity and versatility, offers a wide range of functionalities to handle input/output operations and file handling. Whether you're a beginner taking your first steps in programming or an experienced developer looking to refresh your knowledge, this section will serve as a comprehensive guide to understanding and utilizing input/output and file handling concepts in Python.

Before we dive into the details, let's briefly explore what input/output (I/O) and file handling entail in the context of programming.

Understanding Input/Output and File Handling:

Input/Output (I/O) refers to the communication between a program and its external environment, such as the user, files, or network resources. In Python, I/O is essential for interacting with users, reading data from files, writing data to files, and performing various operations on input and output streams.

File handling, on the other hand, specifically focuses on reading from and writing to files. Files provide a persistent storage mechanism, allowing data to be stored and retrieved across different program executions.

Reading User Input:

Let's start with one of the most fundamental aspects of I/O: reading user input. The "input" function in Python enables you to prompt the user for information and store the provided value in a variable.

```python
name = input("Please enter your name: ")
print("Hello, " + name + "! Welcome to our program.")

# Input: Please enter your name: NS
# Output: Hello, NS! Welcome to our program.
```

In this code snippet, the "input" function displays the prompt "Please enter your name: ", and the user's input is stored in the "name" variable. The program then greets the user using the entered name.

Standard Output and Printing:

Python's "print" function allows you to display information on the standard output, typically the console. It accepts one or more arguments and outputs them as text.

```python
name = "NS"
age = 20
print("Name:", name, "\nAge:", age)
```

```
# Output:
Name: NS
Age: 20

# Here we've used "\n": It's called a new line character.
# It looks good so I've added you do as you want! 😄
```

When executed, this code will display: "Name: NS Age: 20" on
the console if you won't add a new line character; else you
can see how it looks like.

Reading from Files:

To read data from a file, you need to open it in read mode
using the "open" function.

```
file = open("data.txt", "r")
content = file.read()
file.close()
print(content)
```

Here, the file named "data.txt" is opened in read mode ("r"),
and its entire content is read using the "read" method.
Finally, the content is displayed using the "print" function. It's
crucial to close the file using the "close" method after you
finish reading to release system resources. But if you don't
have a file named "data.txt" then either create one or make
the program read from the file you already have.

Else it 'll throw some error, the console will say "what did you think and tried to run, where will I find it, go create one else run the one already you have" 😄 just a small joke! Alright let's move to next one...

Writing to Files:

Similar to reading, you can open a file in write mode ("w") to write data into it.

```
file = open("output.txt", "w")
file.write("Hello, World!")
file.close()
```

In this snippet, the file "output.txt" is opened in write mode, and the text "Hello, World!" is written into it using the "write" method. Remember to close the file after writing to ensure data is saved properly.

Appending to Files:

Appending data to an existing file can be done by opening the file in append mode ("a").

```
file = open("log.txt", "a")
file.write("New log entry.\n")
file.close()
```

This code opens the file "log.txt" in append mode, adds a new log entry, and then closes the file. The "\n" represents a newline character, ensuring each entry is written on a new line. I have already told this before as well.

Context Managers and the "with" Statement:

Python provides a convenient way to handle file operations using context managers and the "with" statement. Context managers automatically handle resource allocation and deallocation. Let's see how this can simplify our file handling code:

```python
with open("data.txt", "r") as file:
    content = file.read()
    print(content)
```

In this example, the "with" statement takes care of opening the file, and the file handle is assigned to the "file" variable. Once the indented block of code is executed, the file is automatically closed, regardless of whether an exception occurs.

In this beginner-friendly guide, we've covered the basics of input/output and file handling in Python. You've learned how to read user input, output text to the console, read from files, write to files, and append data to existing files. Remember to close files after use or utilize the "with" statement for automatic handling.

Python's I/O and file handling capabilities are vital for building interactive applications, processing large datasets, and persisting information. By mastering these concepts, you'll gain the necessary skills to develop powerful Python programs.

As you continue your journey in programming, don't hesitate to explore advanced techniques, such as handling CSV files, working with binary data, or leveraging external libraries like pandas. Python's rich ecosystem provides numerous resources to further enhance your input/output and file handling skills.

2.6. Exception Handling

Exception handling is a vital aspect of any programming language, and Python is no exception (pun intended!). In Python, exceptions are events that occur during the execution of a program, leading to the termination of normal program flow. These exceptions can arise due to a variety of reasons, such as invalid inputs, resource unavailability, or even programming errors. Fortunately, Python provides a robust and flexible mechanism for handling exceptions, allowing developers to gracefully manage errors and ensure the stability and reliability of their applications.

By the end, you will have a solid understanding of how to handle exceptions effectively and write robust code.

1. *The try-except Block:*

The core mechanism for exception handling in Python is the try-except block. It allows you to enclose a block of code that might potentially raise an exception and specify how the program should handle that exception.

```
try:
    # Code that might raise an exception
except ExceptionType:
    # Exception handling code
```

In the above example, the code within the 'try' block is executed. If an exception of type 'ExceptionType' occurs, the execution is immediately transferred to the 'except' block, where the exception is handled. If no exception occurs, the 'except' block is skipped.

2. Catching Multiple Exceptions:

Python allows you to catch multiple exceptions in a single 'except' block by specifying them as a tuple. This feature is useful when different exceptions require similar handling logic.

```
try:
    # Code that might raise an exception
except (ExceptionType1, ExceptionType2):
    # Exception handling code
```

In this case, if either 'ExceptionType1' or 'ExceptionType2' is raised, the code within the 'except' block will be executed.

3. Handling Specific Exceptions:

While catching multiple exceptions can be convenient, sometimes you need to handle each exception differently. Python allows you to have separate 'except' blocks for different exception types.

```
try:
    # Code that might raise an exception
```

```
except ExceptionType1:
    # Exception handling code for ExceptionType1
except ExceptionType2:
    # Exception handling code for ExceptionType2
```

In the above code, if 'ExceptionType1' is raised, the first 'except' block will be executed. If 'ExceptionType1' is raised, the second 'except' block will handle it.

4. The else Clause:

In addition to the 'try' and 'except' blocks, Python provides an optional 'else' clause that can be used to specify code that should be executed only if no exception occurs. This is particularly useful when you want to perform certain actions when your code runs successfully.

```
try:
    # Code that might raise an exception
except ExceptionType:
    # Exception handling code
else:
    # Code to be executed if no exception occurs
```

The code within the 'else' block will only be executed if no exception is raised within the 'try' block.

5. The finally Clause:

Another essential aspect of exception handling in Python is the 'finally' clause. It allows you to specify code that should be executed regardless of whether an exception occurs or not. This ensures that necessary cleanup operations are performed, such as closing files or releasing resources.

```python
try:
    # Code that might raise an exception
except ExceptionType:
    # Exception handling code
finally:
    # Code to be executed regardless of exceptions
```

The 'finally' block is executed even if an exception occurs and is handled within an 'except' block. It is generally used to release resources and perform cleanup operations.

6. Raising Exceptions:

In addition to handling exceptions, Python allows you to raise exceptions explicitly using the 'raise' statement. This can be useful when you encounter a specific condition that warrants an exception to be raised.

```python
def divide(x, y):
    if y == 0:
        raise ZeroDivisionError("Cannot divide by zero")
    return x / y
```

In the above code, if the value of 'y' is 0, a 'ZeroDivisionError' exception is explicitly raised with a custom error message.

7. Custom Exceptions:

Python also enables you to define your custom exceptions by creating a new class that inherits from the 'Exception' class or its subclasses. Custom exceptions can be helpful when you want to provide more specific details about the error or handle specific scenarios differently.

```python
class CustomException(Exception):
    pass


try:
    # Code that might raise a custom exception
except CustomException as e:
    # Exception handling code for CustomException
```

In the above code, if a 'CustomException' is raised, the corresponding 'except' block will handle it.

Exception handling is a crucial aspect of writing reliable and robust Python code. By utilizing try-except blocks, you can gracefully handle exceptions, ensuring that your program continues running smoothly even in the face of errors. The flexibility provided by Python's exception handling mechanism allows you to tailor your error management strategies to suit the specific needs of your application. With the knowledge gained from this article, you are now equipped to handle exceptions effectively and write more resilient Python programs.

Remember, handling exceptions is not just about avoiding program crashes; it is also about providing meaningful feedback to users, logging errors for debugging purposes, and taking appropriate corrective actions. So, embrace the power of exception handling in Python and elevate the quality and reliability of your code!

3. Data Structures:

3.1. LISTS

In the world of programming, data structures play a crucial role in organizing and manipulating data efficiently. One such fundamental data structure in Python is the list. Lists are versatile containers that allow you to store and manage multiple items of different types. In this comprehensive guide, we will explore the ins and outs of lists in Python, discussing their features, operations, and providing code snippets to solidify your understanding.

This is our first section on data sctructures, slowly we'll cover each and every topics in Python, and once completed you will be called a master of Python. It's very exciting ahead. Nothing can be learnt and finished in one night, and nothing can make you an expert of something in one day. Everything needs dedication and time. So, stay tuned and keep implementing.

Understanding Lists:

A list is an ordered collection of items enclosed in square brackets [ ]. These items can be of any data type, such as numbers, strings, or even other lists. Lists are mutable, meaning you can modify their elements after creation. They also support indexing and slicing, allowing you to access specific elements or extract sublists effortlessly.

1. Creating Lists:

To create a list in Python, you simply need to enclose the items within square brackets.

```python
fruits = ['apple', 'banana', 'orange']
```

In the code snippet above, we have created a list called 'fruits' containing three strings: 'apple', 'banana', and 'orange'.

```python
empty_list = []
```

2. Accessing List Elements:

List elements can be accessed using indexing. The index represents the position of an item within the list, starting from 0 for the first element. To access a specific element, you can use the square bracket notation.

```python
fruits = ['apple', 'banana', 'orange']

print(fruits[0])  # Output: apple
print(fruits[1])  # Output: banana
print(fruits[2])  # Output: orange
```

In the code snippet above, we printed the first, second, and third elements of the 'fruits' list by accessing their respective indices.

Modifying List Elements: Lists are mutable, which means you can modify their elements by assigning new values to specific indices.

```
fruits = ['apple', 'banana', 'orange']
fruits[1] = 'mango'
print(fruits)           # Output: ['apple', 'mango', 'orange']
```

In the code snippet above, we modified the second element of the 'fruits' list from 'banana' to 'mango'. The resulting list now reflects the updated value.

3. Appending and Extending Lists:

Lists provide methods to add elements at the end. The 'append()' method allows you to add a single item, while the 'extend()' method allows you to concatenate another list to the existing one.

```
fruits = ['apple', 'banana']
fruits.append('orange')
print(fruits)

# Output: ['apple', 'banana', 'orange']

more_fruits = ['mango', 'watermelon']
fruits.extend(more_fruits)
print(fruits)

# Output: ['apple', 'banana', 'orange', 'mango', 'watermelon']
```

In the code snippet above, we first used the 'append()' method to add the string 'orange' to the 'fruits' list. Then, we created a new list called 'more_fruits' and used the 'extend()' method to concatenate it to the 'fruits' list.

4. *Slicing Lists:*

Lists support slicing, allowing you to extract sublists based on indices. The slicing syntax involves specifying the start index, end index (exclusive), and an optional step value.

```python
fruits = ['apple', 'banana', 'orange', 'mango', 'watermelon']

print(fruits[1:4])     # Output: ['banana', 'orange', 'mango']
print(fruits[:3])      # Output: ['apple', 'banana', 'orange']
print(fruits[2:])      # Output: ['orange', 'mango',
'watermelon']
print(fruits[::2])     # Output: ['apple', 'orange',
'watermelon']


print(fruits[::-1])
# Output: ['watermelon', 'mango', 'orange', 'banana',
'apple']
```

In the code snippet above, we demonstrated various slicing operations on the 'fruits' list. By specifying the start and end indices, we extracted different sublists. Additionally, we used the step value to skip elements in the sublist.

**Common List Operations:**

Apart from basic operations, lists in Python offer a wide range of methods to manipulate and work with the data they hold. Let's discuss about a few commonly used list operations:

- len(): Returns the number of elements in a list.
- index(): Returns the index of the first occurrence of a specified element.
- count(): Returns the number of occurrences of a specified element.
- sort(): Sorts the elements of the list in ascending order.
- reverse(): Reverses the order of elements in the list.

Let's understand this by writing the code:

```python
numbers = [5, 9, 2, 7, 8, 3, 1, 7, 4, 6]

print(len(numbers))      # Output: 10
print(numbers.index(3))   # Output: 5
print(numbers.count(7))   # Output: 2

numbers.sort()
print(numbers)           # Output: [1, 2, 3, 4, 5, 6, 7, 7, 8, 9]

numbers.reverse()
print(numbers)           # Output: [9, 8, 7, 7, 6, 5, 4, 3, 2, 1]
```

After covering the basics of lists, there are a few additional points that beginners should know to enhance their understanding and usage of lists in Python:

5. Nested Lists:

Lists can contain other lists as elements, creating a nested structure. This allows you to create multidimensional data structures or represent hierarchical relationships.

```python
matrix = [[1, 2, 3], [4, 5, 6], [7, 8, 9]]
print(matrix[0][1])              # Output: 2
```

In the code snippet above, we created a nested list called 'matrix' where each element is itself a list. Accessing individual elements within the nested list involves using multiple indices.

6. List Comprehensions:

List comprehensions provide a concise way to create new lists based on existing lists. They allow you to combine loops and conditional statements in a single line of code.

```python
numbers = [1, 2, 3, 4, 5]
squares = [x ** 2 for x in numbers]
print(squares)                # Output: [1, 4, 9, 16, 25]
```

In the code snippet above, we used a list comprehension to create a new list called 'squares' where each element is the square of the corresponding element in the 'numbers' list.

7. Aliasing and Cloning:

When working with lists, it's important to understand the concepts of aliasing and cloning. Aliasing occurs when two or more variables refer to the same list object. Modifying one variable will affect all the aliases. To create a copy of a list without aliasing, you can use the 'copy()' method or slice notation.

```python
fruits = ['apple', 'banana', 'orange']
alias = fruits
alias.append('mango')
print(fruits)  # Output: ['apple', 'banana', 'orange', 'mango']

clone = fruits.copy()
clone.append('watermelon')
print(fruits)  # Output: ['apple', 'banana', 'orange', 'grape']
print(clone)
# Output: ['apple', 'banana', 'orange', 'grape', 'watermelon']
```

In the code snippet above, we demonstrated how modifying the 'alias' list affects the 'fruits' list, as they refer to the same object. On the other hand, the 'clone' list, created using the 'copy()' method, remains separate from the original list. And your original list is safe.

8. *List Mutability and Immutability:*

While lists are mutable, meaning their elements can be modified, some elements within a list may be immutable. For example, if a list contains string elements, the individual characters of the strings cannot be modified directly. To modify the characters, you would need to create a new string and assign it to the list element.

```python
names = ['Nibe', 'Dita', 'NS']
names[0] = 'Nibe'
print(names)  # Output: ['Nibe', 'Dita', 'NS']


names[1][0] = 'N'

# Error: Strings are immutable
# TypeError: 'str' object does not support item assignment
```

In the code snippet above, we successfully modified the first element of the 'names' list but encountered an error when trying to modify the first character of the second element. To overcome this, you would need to create a new string and replace the entire element as Strings are immutable.

Lists are incredibly versatile and powerful, allowing you to tackle a wide range of data manipulation tasks. Remember to practice regularly and explore further to become proficient in working with lists and other data structures in Python.

Lists are fundamental data structures in Python that allow you to store and manipulate collections of items. Understanding how to create, access, modify, and perform operations on lists is essential for every programmer.

We covered the basics of lists, including their creation, element access, modification, appending, extending, slicing, some common operations and some additional points: Nested Lists, List Comprehensions, Aliasing and Cloning, List Mutability and Immutability, etc. Armed with this knowledge, you can confidently leverage lists to handle complex data in your Python programs. Keep practicing and exploring the vast possibilities offered by lists, and you'll become a proficient Python programmer in no time.

3.2. TUPLES

In the realm of Python programming, tuples are a versatile and valuable data structure. They offer a range of features that make them indispensable for various programming tasks. In this article, we will explore tuples in-depth, discussing their definition, properties, operations, and use cases. Whether you are a beginner or an experienced Python developer, this comprehensive guide will enhance your understanding of tuples and their significance within data structures.

Don't hurry! We'll go in a flow and slowly with the best understanding way we'll complete the journey from novice to pro and become a Master of Python. Have some patience and practice daily! So, let's go...

What are Tuples?

A tuple is an ordered, immutable collection of objects in Python. It is similar to a list but with one crucial distinction: tuples cannot be modified once they are created. This immutability grants them certain advantages over other data structures in specific scenarios. Tuples are created by enclosing comma-separated values within parentheses.

```
my_tuple = (1, 2, 3, 4, 5)
```

Properties of Tuples

1. Immutable Nature:

As i mentioned earlier, tuples are immutable, meaning their values cannot be changed after creation. This immutability ensures data integrity and prevents accidental modifications. While this might seem restrictive at first, it offers advantages such as faster processing and the ability to use tuples as dictionary keys.

2. Ordered Elements:

Tuples maintain the order of elements, preserving the sequence in which they were defined. This characteristic allows us to access tuple elements by their index, just like we would with lists.

```
my_tuple = (1, 2, 3)
print(my_tuple[0])  # Output: 1
```

3. Heterogeneous Data Types:

Tuples can contain elements of different data types. This versatility allows developers to store diverse information within a single tuple. Here's an example demonstrating a tuple with mixed data types:

```
person_details = ("Nibedita Sahu", 25,
"nibe@example.com")
```

Basic Operations on Tuples

1. Accessing Elements:

As tuples preserve order, individual elements can be accessed using indexing or slicing.

```python
my_tuple = (1, 2, 3, 4, 5)
print(my_tuple[2])        # Output: 3

print(my_tuple[1:4])      # Output: (2, 3, 4)
```

2. Concatenation:

Tuples can be concatenated using the '+' operator, creating a new tuple containing the combined elements.

```python
tuple1 = (1, 2, 3)
tuple2 = (4, 5, 6)
concatenated_tuple = tuple1 + tuple2
print(concatenated_tuple)        # Output: (1, 2, 3, 4, 5, 6)
```

3. Multiplication:

Tuples can be multiplied by an integer, resulting in a new tuple with repeated elements.

```python
my_tuple = (1, 2)
multiplied_tuple = my_tuple * 3
print(multiplied_tuple)          # Output: (1, 2, 1, 2, 1, 2)
```

4. Length of a Tuple:

The 'len()' function can be used to determine the number of elements in a tuple. Or you can say "to know the length of the tuple."

```python
my_tuple = (1, 2, 3, 4, 5)
print(len(my_tuple))           # Output: 5
```

Use Cases and Benefits of Tuples

1. Unpacking Values:

Tuples enable the convenient unpacking of multiple values in a single assignment statement. This feature is particularly useful when dealing with functions that return multiple values.

```python
def get_name_and_age():
    return "Nibedita Sahu", 20

name, age = get_name_and_age()
print(name)                # Output: Nibedita Sahu
print(age)                 # Output: 20

# Or directly in one line you can print both name and age
as you like!
print(name, age)           # Output: Nibedita Sahu 20
```

- ***Dictionary Keys:*** As tuples are immutable, they can be used as keys in dictionaries. Lists, which are mutable, cannot be used as keys. This property allows tuples to serve as reliable and efficient identifiers in dictionary-based data structures.
- ***Function Arguments:*** Tuples can be employed to pass multiple values as arguments to functions. This is beneficial when the number of arguments is fixed, and the order of values is significant.
- ***Lightweight Data Structures:*** Compared to lists, tuples consume less memory due to their immutability. This makes them ideal for scenarios where data integrity and memory efficiency are essential.

Additional Points to Enhance Your Understanding of Tuples

1. Iterating Over a Tuple:

Tuples can be easily iterated using loops, such as the 'for' loop, to access each element sequentially.

```python
my_tuple = (1, 2, 3, 4, 5)
for item in my_tuple:
    print(item, end=" ")      # Output:1 2 3 4 5
```

```python
# Or if you don't want it in one line then you can remove it
as well.
for num in my_tuple:
print(num)

# Output:
1
2
3
4
5
```

It's upto you, how you like it and how you want it. That's why Python has so much fun dude! 'end=' is nothing too much complicated, it means how you want to finish the end. Here I wanted the numbers to come in a single line with space separated, so I gave a space for it. Modify it according to your mood!

2. *Tuple Packing and Unpacking:*

Tuple packing refers to combining multiple values into a single tuple, while tuple unpacking allows us to assign those values to separate variables. This feature provides a convenient way to group related data.

```python
person = "Nibedita Sahu"
age = 20
email = "nibe@example.com"
```

```python
# Tuple packing
person_details = person, age, email

# Tuple unpacking
name, age, email = person_details

print(name)        # Output: Nibedita Sahu
print(age)        # Output: 20
print(email)        # Output: nibe@example.com
```

3. Nested Tuples:

Tuples can be nested within other tuples, allowing for the creation of complex data structures. This nesting can be done to any level, providing flexibility in representing hierarchical or multi-dimensional data.

```python
nested_tuple = ((1, 2, 3), (4, 5, 6), (7, 8, 9))
print(nested_tuple[1])        # Output: (4, 5, 6)
print(nested_tuple[1][2])        # Output: 6
```

4. Tuple Comparison:

Tuples support comparison operations, such as equality (==), inequality (!=), greater than (>), less than (<), etc. The comparison is performed elementwise from left to right until a mismatch is found or the end of the tuple is reached.

```python
tuple1 = (1, 2, 3)
tuple2 = (1, 2, 4)

print(tuple1 == tuple2)        # Output: False
```

```
print(tuple1 < tuple2)          # Output: True
print(tuple1 > tuple2)          # Output: False
```

- **_Tuple Methods:_** Tuples have a few built-in methods that provide additional functionality. Some of these methods include 'count()' and 'index()'. The 'count()' method returns the number of occurrences of a specific value within the tuple, while the 'index()' method returns the index of the first occurrence of a given value.

```
my_tuple = (1, 2, 2, 3, 4, 2)

print(my_tuple.count(2))              # Output: 3
print(my_tuple.index(3))              # Output: 3
```

5. Type Conversion:

Tuples can be converted to other data structures using built-in conversion functions. For example, 'list(my_tuple)' will convert a tuple into a list, and 'set(my_tuple)' will convert it into a set. This flexibility allows for seamless interconversion between different data structures as per the requirements of your program.

By delving into the world of tuples, you have acquired a solid foundation in understanding their properties, operations, and use cases. You now possess the knowledge to leverage tuples efficiently in your Python programs, whether it is for grouping related data, creating lightweight data structures, or passing multiple arguments to functions. Tuples offer immutability, order, and compatibility with various Python features, making them an invaluable tool for any Python developer.

Remember, practice is key to mastering tuples and other data structures. Regularly incorporating tuples into your coding exercises and projects will not only reinforce your understanding but also enhance your overall Python programming skills.

3.3. DICTIONARIES

Data structures play a vital role in computer programming, allowing us to efficiently store, organize, and retrieve data. Among these structures, dictionaries stand out as one of the most versatile and powerful options. In this section, we'll delve into dictionaries as a data structure in Python, understanding their unique properties, how they work, and their practical applications. Whether you're a beginner or an experienced programmer, this guide will help you grasp the fundamentals of dictionaries and harness their full potential.

Understanding Dictionaries

A dictionary in Python is a collection that holds key-value pairs. Unlike lists or arrays, where elements are accessed using integer indices, dictionaries allow us to access elements using their associated keys. Think of a dictionary as a real-life language dictionary, where words (keys) have corresponding meanings (values).

Creating a dictionary is straightforward in Python. You use curly braces '{}' and separate each key-value pair with a colon ':'.

```python
# Creating a dictionary of student grades
student_grades = {'Nibedita': 85, 'Tushar': 82, 'Salil': 88,
'Mayukh': 91}
```

In this case, 'Nibedita', 'Tushar', 'Salil', and 'Mayukh' are the keys, while 85, 82, 88, and 91 are the corresponding values.

Accessing Values in Dictionaries:

Dictionaries allow us to retrieve values by specifying the associated key in square brackets '[]'.

```python
# Accessing 'Nibedita's grade
nibedita_grade = student_grades['Nibedita']
print(nibedita_grade)              # Output: 85
```

Note that if you attempt to access a key that doesn't exist in the dictionary, Python will raise a 'KeyError' exception. To avoid this, you can use the 'get()' method, which returns a default value if the key is not found.

```python
# Let's use get() to access a key safely
bidisha_grade = student_grades.get('Bidisha', 'N/A')
print(bidisha_grade)               # Output: 'N/A'


# Or if you won't keep anything then it'll give you None.
bidisha_grade = student_grades.get('Bidisha')
print(bidisha_grade)               # Output: None
```

Updating and Adding Entries:

Dictionaries are mutable, meaning you can modify their contents even after creation. To update the value associated with a key, simply use its corresponding key and assign a new value.

```
# Let's update Nibedita's grade
student_grades['Nibedita'] = 89
```

- To add a new entry to the dictionary, assign a value to a new key:

```
# Adding a new student and grade
student_grades['Nibe'] = 94
```

Iterating over Dictionaries:

Dictionaries offer various methods for traversing their elements. One common approach is to use a for loop with the 'items()' method, which returns a view object containing key-value pairs as tuples.

```
# Iterating over dictionary using items()
for student, grade in student_grades.items():
    print(student, grade)


# Output:
Nibedita 89
Tushar 82
Salil 88
Mayukh 91
Nibe 94
```

Alternatively, you can iterate over keys or values separately using the 'keys()' and 'values()' methods, respectively.

Checking if a Key Exists:

Before accessing a key, it's often useful to check if it exists in the dictionary to avoid errors. The 'in' keyword can be used for this purpose.

```python
# Checking if a key exists
if 'Tushar' in student_grades:
    print("Tushar's grade: ", student_grades['Tushar'])


# Output: Tushar's grade: 82
```

Removing Entries:

To remove a key-value pair from a dictionary, you can use the 'del' keyword followed by the key:

```python
print(student_grades)
# Output:
{'Nibedita': 89, 'Tushar': 82, 'Salil': 88, 'Mayukh': 91, 'Nibe':
94}

# Removing 'Nibe':
del student_grades['Nibe']
print(student_grades)
```

```
# Output: {'Nibedita': 89, 'Tushar': 82, 'Salil': 88, 'Mayukh':
91}
```

Dictionary Operations:

Dictionaries support several operations beyond basic manipulation

Copying a dictionary: You can create a shallow copy of a dictionary using the 'copy()' method or the built-in 'dict()' constructor.

```
# Copying a dictionary
copied_dict = student_grades.copy()
```

Checking the length: The 'len()' function returns the number of key-value pairs in a dictionary.

```
# Checking the length of a dictionary
num_students = len(student_grades)
```

Clearing a dictionary: The 'clear()' method removes all key-value pairs from a dictionary, making it empty.

```
# Clearing a dictionary
student_grades.clear()
```

Checking equality: Dictionaries can be compared for equality using the '==' operator, which checks if the key-value pairs match.

```python
# Checking equality of dictionaries
dict1 = {'a': 1, 'b': 2}
dict2 = {'b': 2, 'a': 1}

print(dict1 == dict2)        # Output: True
```

Nested Dictionaries:

Dictionaries can be nested within other dictionaries, allowing for complex data structures. This is useful when dealing with hierarchical data.

```python
# Nested dictionaries
student_details = {
    'Nibe': {'age': 20, 'major': 'Mathematics'},
    'Dita': {'age': 21, 'major': 'Data Science'}
}

print(student_details['Nibe']['major'])        # Output:
'Mathematics'
```

- ***Practical Applications of Dictionaries:*** Dictionaries find practical applications in a wide range of programming scenarios, including:

- ***Data Retrieval:*** Dictionaries enable efficient data retrieval using keys. This makes them suitable for scenarios such as database lookups or caching.

- ***Configuration Management:*** Dictionaries serve as a convenient way to store and manage configurations for applications, with keys representing specific settings and values holding their corresponding values.

- ***Counting and Frequency Analysis:*** Dictionaries excel at counting occurrences of elements in a collection. Each element can be stored as a key, and the associated value can represent the count.

```python
# Counting occurrences of elements
word = 'Hello'
count = {}

for char in word:
    count[char] = count.get(char, 0) + 1

print(count)  # Output: {'H': 1, 'e': 1, 'l': 2, 'o': 1}
```

1. Mapping Relationships:

Dictionaries allow for mapping relationships between different entities. For instance, dictionaries can be used to establish connections between users and their corresponding preferences.

After covering the basics of dictionaries in data structures, beginners can further expand their knowledge and skills by exploring the following concepts:

Dictionary Methods: Python dictionaries come with a variety of built-in methods that provide additional functionality. Some commonly used methods include:

- ***keys():*** Returns a view object containing all the keys in the dictionary.
- ***values():*** Returns a view object containing all the values in the dictionary.
- ***items():*** Returns a view object containing all the key-value pairs as tuples.
- ***pop():*** Removes and returns the value associated with a given key.
- ***update():*** Updates a dictionary with key-value pairs from another dictionary or iterable.
- ***clear():*** Removes all the key-value pairs from the dictionary.

```python
student_grades = {'Nibedita': 85, 'Tushar': 82, 'Salil': 86, 'Mayukh': 91}

# Getting the keys
```

```python
keys = student_grades.keys()
print(keys)  # Output: dict_keys(['Nibedita', 'Tushar', 'Salil',
'Mayukh'])

# Getting the values
values = student_grades.values()
print(values)  # Output: dict_values([85, 82, 86, 91])

# Getting the key-value pairs
items = student_grades.items()
print(items)  # Output: dict_items([('Nibedita', 85), ('Tushar',
82), ('Salil', 86), ('Mayukh', 91)])

# Removing a key-value pair
grade = student_grades.pop('Nibedita')
print(grade)  # Output: 85

# Updating the dictionary
student_grades.update({'Salil': 88})
print(student_grades)  # Output: {'Tushar': 82, 'Salil': 88,
'Mayukh': 91}
```

2. *Dictionary Comprehension:*

Similar to list comprehension, dictionary comprehension
provides a concise way to create dictionaries based on
iterable objects. It involves specifying key-value pairs and an
optional condition.

```python
numbers = [1, 2, 3, 4, 5]
squares = {x: x ** 2 for x in numbers}
```

```
print(squares)  # Output: {1: 1, 2: 4, 3: 9, 4: 16, 5: 25}
```

3. *Dictionary Sorting:*

By default, dictionaries in Python are unordered. However, if you need to sort a dictionary based on keys or values, you can use the 'sorted()' function along with the 'items()' method.

```python
student_grades = {'Nibedita': 85, 'Tushar': 82, 'Salil': 88, 'Mayukh': 91}

# Sorting by keys
sorted_grades_by_key = dict(sorted(student_grades.items()))

# Sorting by values
sorted_grades_by_value = dict(sorted(student_grades.items(), key=lambda x: x[1]))

print(sorted_grades_by_key)    # Output: {'Mayukh': 91, 'Nibedita': 85, 'Salil': 88, 'Tushar': 82}
print(sorted_grades_by_value)  # Output: {'Tushar': 82, 'Nibedita': 85, 'Salil': 88, 'Mayukh': 91}
```

4. *Handling Missing Keys:*

When accessing a key that doesn't exist in a dictionary, Python raises a 'KeyError' by default. However, you can use the 'defaultdict' class from the 'collections' module to handle missing keys gracefully.

```python
from collections import defaultdict

student_grades = defaultdict(lambda: 'N/A')
student_grades['Tushar'] = 89


print("Tushar's grade: ", student_grades['Tushar'])   #
Output: Tushar's grade:  89
print("Nidisha's grade: ", student_grades['Bidisha'])  #
Output: Bidisha's grade:  N/A
```

5. *Dictionary Views:*

Dictionary views provide dynamic and live views of the keys, values, or key-value pairs in a dictionary. They reflect any changes made to the dictionary.

```python
student_grades = {'Nibedita': 85, 'Tushar': 82, 'Salil': 88, 'Mayukh': 91}

keys_view = student_grades.keys()
values_view = student_grades.values()
items_view = student_grades.items()

# Modifying the dictionary
student_grades['Bidisha'] = 81

print(keys_view)
 # Output: dict_keys(['Nibedita', 'Tushar', 'Salil', 'Mayukh', 'Bidisha'])


print(values_view)
# Output: dict_values([85, 82, 88, 91, 81])
```

```
print(items_view)
# Output: dict_items([('Nibedita', 85), ('Tushar', 82), ('Salil',
88), ('Mayukh', 91), ('Bidisha', 81)])
```

By exploring these additional concepts, you can enhance your understanding of dictionaries in data structures and broaden your ability to leverage dictionaries effectively in Python programming. Dictionaries are a versatile tool that can handle various real-world scenarios and mastering them will significantly contribute to your coding skills.

3.4. SETS AND FROZENSETS

When working with data in Python, it is crucial to understand
the various data structures available. One such data structure
is a set, which is a collection of unique elements. In this
section, we will explore sets in data structures and how they
can be used effectively in Python.

Introduction to Sets

A set is an unordered collection of unique elements in
Python. Unlike lists or tuples, sets do not allow duplicate
values. The elements in a set are enclosed within curly braces
'{}' and are separated by commas.

```
fruits = {"apple", "banana", "orange", "apple"}
print(fruits)      # Output: {'banana', 'orange', 'apple'}
```

In this example, we have defined a set called 'fruits' with four
elements: "apple", "banana", "orange", and "apple".
However, when we print the set, we will notice that the
duplicate element "apple" is only displayed once. This is
because sets automatically eliminate duplicate values. Or you
may have studied it in Math as well in school about the sets.

Set Operations

Sets in Python support various operations that can be performed on them. Let's explore some of the commonly used operations:

1. Adding Elements:

We can add elements to a set using the 'add()' method.

```python
fruits = {"apple", "banana", "orange"}
fruits.add("mango")
print(fruits)
# Output: {'apple', 'mango', 'orange', 'banana'}
```

2. Removing Elements:

To remove an element from a set, we can use the 'remove()' method. If the element is not found in the set, a 'KeyError' is raised. Alternatively, we can use the 'discard()' method, which does not raise an error if the element is not present.

```python
fruits = {"apple", "banana", "orange"}
fruits.remove("banana")
print(fruits)         # Output: {'apple', 'orange'}
fruits = {"apple", "banana", "orange"}
fruits.remove("cherry")
print(fruits)         # Output: KeyError: 'cherry'
fruits = {"apple", "banana", "orange"}
fruits.discard("cherry")
print(fruits)         # Output: {'orange', 'apple', 'banana'}
```

3. _Mathematical Operations:_

Sets support various mathematical operations such as union, intersection, and difference. These operations can be performed using built-in methods or operators.

```python
#Union:
set1 = {1, 2, 3}
set2 = {3, 4, 5}
union_set = set1.union(set2)
print(union_set)           # Output: {1, 2, 3, 4, 5}
Intersection:
set1 = {1, 2, 3}
set2 = {3, 4, 5}
intersection_set = set1.intersection(set2)
print(intersection_set)       # Output: {3}
Difference:
set1 = {1, 2, 3}
set2 = {3, 4, 5}
difference_set = set1.difference(set2)
print(difference_set)        # Output: {1, 2}
```

4. _Membership Test:_

We can check if an element exists in a set using the 'in' keyword.

```python
fruits = {"apple", "banana", "orange"}
print("apple" in fruits)       # Output: True
print("mango" in fruits)       # Output: False
```

Sets are particularly useful when dealing with large datasets and need to quickly check for the existence of elements.

Applications of Sets

Sets find applications in various scenarios, such as:

1. Removing Duplicates:

Sets can be used to remove duplicate elements from a list or any other collection. We can convert the collection to a set and then back to a list, which automatically eliminates the duplicates.

```
numbers = [1, 2, 3, 2, 4, 5, 1]
unique_numbers = list(set(numbers))
print(unique_numbers)              # Output: [1, 2, 3, 4, 5]
```

2. Mathematical Operations:

Sets can be used to perform mathematical operations, such as finding the common elements between two sets, finding the distinct elements, and more. These operations are highly efficient with sets.

3. Membership Testing:

Sets provide a fast way to check whether an element is present in a collection. This is useful when working with large datasets and need to quickly search for specific values.

Some additional points that a beginner should learn about sets in Data Structures after understanding the basics we've discussed above...

1. Set Membership and Iteration:

Sets allow for efficient membership testing using the 'in' keyword, as demonstrated earlier. Additionally, sets can be iterated using loops, just like other iterable objects in Python. This allows you to perform operations on each element in the set easily.

```
fruits = {"apple", "banana", "orange"}
for fruit in fruits:
    print(fruit)

# Output:
orange
banana
apple
```

2. Immutable Elements:

Sets in Python can only contain elements that are immutable, such as numbers, strings, and tuples. Mutable objects like lists and dictionaries cannot be elements of a set. This is because sets use hashing to quickly determine uniqueness and mutable objects can change their hash value, leading to unexpected behavior.

3. Frozen Sets:

While sets are mutable, Python also provides a built-in immutable variant called frozen sets. Frozen sets can be created using the 'frozenset()' function and have the same properties as sets, except that they cannot be modified once created. Frozen sets are useful in situations where you need an immutable collection of unique elements.

```python
numbers = frozenset([1, 2, 3, 4])
print(numbers)            # Output: frozenset({1, 2, 3, 4})
```

4. Set Comprehension:

Similar to list comprehensions, Python also supports set comprehensions, which allow you to create sets using a concise syntax. Set comprehensions are enclosed in curly braces and follow a similar pattern as list comprehensions.

```python
squares = {x**2 for x in range(1, 6)}
print(squares)            # Output: {1, 4, 9, 16, 25}
```

5. Performance Characteristics:

Sets in Python are implemented as hash tables, which provide fast average-case performance for common operations such as membership testing, adding elements, and removing elements. However, the performance can degrade in the worst-case scenario when there are many hash collisions. It's important to be aware of the underlying performance characteristics when working with sets and to consider the specific use case.

6. Set Operations and Methods:

Sets in Python provide a wide range of operations and methods that allow you to manipulate and analyze sets efficiently. Some commonly used methods include 'update()' , 'clear()', 'copy()', 'issubset()', 'issuperset()', and 'symmetric_difference()'. It's beneficial to explore the full set of methods available and understand their functionality to maximize the usefulness of sets in your programs.

Sets are a valuable data structure in Python when working with unique elements. They provide efficient operations for adding, removing, and performing mathematical operations on elements.

With their ability to eliminate duplicates and fast membership testing, sets are highly useful in various scenarios. By understanding sets and their operations, you can write more efficient and clean Python code.

By mastering the additional points, beginners and even skilled professionals will have a solid understanding of sets in data structures and be equipped to utilize them effectively in Python.

Remember to use sets whenever you need to deal with collections of unique elements and leverage their powerful features to simplify your programming tasks.

3.5. Arrays (NumPy)

Data structures play a vital role in computer science and programming, as they allow us to efficiently organize and manipulate data. One such data structure is an array. Arrays are fundamental in many programming languages, including Python, and they provide a convenient and efficient way to store and manipulate large amounts of data.

In Python, the NumPy library (Numerical Python) is widely used for working with arrays. NumPy provides a powerful and efficient implementation of multidimensional arrays, along with a collection of functions for mathematical operations on arrays. In this article, we are going to explore arrays in the context of NumPy, discussing their features, advantages, and how to work with them effectively.

What are Arrays?

An array is a collection of elements of the same type, organized in a contiguous block of memory. Each element in the array is accessed by its index, which represents its position in the array. Arrays provide efficient random access to elements, allowing constant-time access to any element.

In Python, arrays can be created using the NumPy library. NumPy arrays are homogeneous, meaning they can only store elements of the same data type. This ensures efficient memory usage and enables vectorized operations, which significantly enhance the performance of numerical computations.

Creating Arrays

To work with arrays in NumPy, we first need to import the NumPy library. We can then create arrays using the 'numpy.array()' function by passing a Python list or tuple as an argument.

```
import numpy as np

# Creating a 1D array
arr_1d = np.array([1, 2, 3, 4, 5])
print(arr_1d)              # Output: [1 2 3 4 5]

# Creating a 2D array
arr_2d = np.array([[1, 2, 3], [4, 5, 6]])
print(arr_2d)

# Output:
[[1 2 3]
 [4 5 6]]
```

In the example above, we created a 1D array 'arr_1d' and a 2D array 'arr_2d' using the 'numpy.array()' function. We pass a list of elements to the function, which creates the corresponding array.

Array Attributes

Arrays in NumPy have several important attributes that provide useful information about the array. Some commonly used attributes include:

- **_'ndim':_** Returns the number of dimensions of the array.
- **_'shape':_** Returns a tuple representing the size of each dimension of the array.
- **_'size':_** Returns the total number of elements in the array.
- **_'dtype':_** Returns the data type of the elements in the array.
- **_'itemsize':_** Returns the size (in bytes) of each element in the array.
- **_'nbytes':_** Returns the total size (in bytes) of the array.

```
import numpy as np

arr = np.array([[1, 2, 3], [4, 5, 6]])

print("Shape:", arr.shape)
print("Number of dimensions:", arr.ndim)
print("Size:", arr.size)
print("Data type:", arr.dtype)
print("Size of each element (in bytes):", arr.itemsize)
print("Total size of the array (in bytes):", arr.nbytes)
```

```
# Output:
Shape: (2, 3)
Number of dimensions: 2
Size: 6
Data type: int32
Size of each element (in bytes): 4
Total size of the array (in bytes): 24
```

In the example above, we create a 2D array 'arr' and then print its attributes. We can see that the shape of the array is '(2, 3)', indicating that it has 2 rows and 3 columns. The array has 2 dimensions, a total of 6 elements, and each element is of type 'int64'. The size of each element is 8 bytes, and the total size of the array is 48 bytes.

Array Indexing and Slicing

Accessing and manipulating array elements is a common operation when working with arrays. In NumPy, we can use indexing and slicing techniques to retrieve specific elements or subarrays from an array.

Indexing in NumPy starts from 0, similar to other programming languages. We can access elements of a 1D array using their index, and elements of a 2D array using row and column indices.

```
import numpy as np
```

```python
arr = np.array([1, 2, 3, 4, 5])
print("First element:", arr[0])
print("Last element:", arr[-1])

# Output:
First element: 1
Last element: 5


arr = np.array([[1, 2, 3], [4, 5, 6]])
print("Element at (0, 1):", arr[0, 1])
print("First row:", arr[0, :])

# Output:
Element at (0, 1): 2
First row: [1 2 3]
```

In the above example, we create a 1D array 'arr' and print the first and last elements using indexing. We also create a 2D array 'arr' and access specific elements using row and column indices.

Slicing allows us to extract subarrays from a larger array by specifying the start and end indices along with an optional step size. Slicing works similarly for both 1D and 2D arrays.

```python
import numpy as np

arr = np.array([1, 2, 3, 4, 5])
```

```python
print("Slice from index 1 to 3:", arr[1:4])
print("Every alternate element:", arr[::2])

# Output:
Slice from index 1 to 3: [2 3 4]
Every alternate element: [1 3 5]


arr = np.array([[1, 2, 3], [4, 5, 6], [7, 8, 9]])
print(arr[1:3, 0:2])

# Output:
[[4 5]
 [7 8]]
```

In the example above, we create a 1D array 'arr' and perform slicing operations to extract specific elements or subarrays. We also create a 2D array 'arr' and slice it to obtain a subarray consisting of rows 1 to 2 and columns 0 to 1.

Array Operations

NumPy provides a wide range of mathematical functions and operators that can be applied to arrays. These functions and operators are designed to work efficiently on arrays, thanks to NumPy's underlying implementation.

Element-wise Operations

Element-wise operations apply a specific operation to each element of an array. This can be done using the arithmetic operators provided by NumPy, such as '+', '-', '*', '/', and others. These operators perform the corresponding operation on each element of the array, resulting in a new array of the same shape.

```python
import numpy as np


arr = np.array([1, 2, 3, 4, 5])
result = arr * 2
print("Result:", result)        # Output: Result: [ 2  4  6  8 10]



arr1 = np.array([1, 2, 3])
arr2 = np.array([4, 5, 6])
result = arr1 + arr2
print("Result:", result)        # Output: Result: [5 7 9]
```

In the example above, we create a 1D array 'arr' and multiply it by 2 using the '*' operator. We also create two 1D arrays, 'arr1' and 'arr2', and perform element-wise addition using the '+' operator.

Array Functions

NumPy provides a rich set of mathematical functions that can be applied to arrays. These functions operate on the entire array or along a specified axis, allowing for efficient computation of various statistics and mathematical operations.

```python
import numpy as np

arr = np.array([1, 2, 3, 4, 5])
print("Sum of elements:", np.sum(arr))
print("Mean of elements:", np.mean(arr))
print("Maximum element:", np.max(arr))
print("Minimum element:", np.min(arr))


# Output:
Sum of elements: 15
Mean of elements: 3.0
Maximum element: 5
Minimum element: 1



arr = np.array([[1, 2, 3], [4, 5, 6]])
print("Sum along rows:", np.sum(arr, axis=0))
print("Sum along columns:", np.sum(arr, axis=1))

# Output:
Sum along rows: [5 7 9]
Sum along columns: [ 6 15]
```

In the example above, we compute various statistics for a 1D array 'arr', such as the sum, mean, maximum, and minimum. We also compute the sum along rows and columns for a 2D array 'arr' using the 'axis' parameter.

<u>***Advantages of Arrays (NumPy)***</u>

Using arrays from the NumPy library offers several advantages over regular Python lists. Some key advantages are as follows:

- ***Efficiency:*** NumPy arrays are implemented in C, providing superior performance compared to pure Python lists. This is particularly important when working with large datasets or performing intensive numerical computations.

- ***Ease of use:*** NumPy provides a wide range of functions and operators specifically designed for array operations. This simplifies the code and makes it more readable and concise.

- ***Memory efficiency:*** NumPy arrays are homogeneous, meaning they require less memory compared to Python lists. This is particularly important when dealing with large datasets, as it allows for efficient storage and manipulation of data.

- ***Vectorized operations:*** NumPy enables vectorized operations, which apply an operation to an entire array instead of looping over individual elements. This significantly improves computational efficiency and reduces code complexity.

Arrays (NumPy) are a fundamental data structure in Python for efficiently storing and manipulating large amounts of data. The NumPy library provides a powerful implementation of arrays along with a collection of functions for mathematical operations. Understanding how to create, index, slice, and perform operations on arrays is essential for working with data in Python effectively. By harnessing the advantages of NumPy arrays, developers can write efficient and concise code for numerical computations and data analysis tasks.

3.6. Series and DataFrames (Pandas)

When working with data in Python, one of the most popular libraries to manipulate and analyze data is Pandas. Pandas provides two main data structures: Series and DataFrames. These data structures are essential for handling and processing structured data efficiently.

In this section, we will explore Series and DataFrames in detail, understanding their characteristics, and how they can be used effectively in data manipulation tasks.

Series

A Series is a one-dimensional labeled array that can hold any data type. It is similar to a column in a spreadsheet or a SQL table. Each element in a Series has a unique label called an index. The index helps in accessing and manipulating data efficiently.

To create a Series, we can use the 'pd.Series()' function in Pandas.

```
import pandas as pd

# Create a Series of siblings' scores
```

```
scores = pd.Series([90, 85, 92, 99, 81])
```

In the code snippet above, we imported the Pandas library and created a Series called 'scores' with five elements. By default, the index labels are assigned as integers starting from 0. We can access elements in a Series using these index labels.

```
# Accessing elements in a Series
print(scores[0])              # Output: 90
print(scores[2])              # Output: 92
```

We can also assign custom index labels to the Series elements.

```
# Create a Series with custom index labels
scores = pd.Series([90, 85, 92, 99, 81],
        index=['Nibedita', 'Tushar', 'Salil', 'Mayukh',
'Bidisha'])

# Accessing elements using custom index labels
print(scores['Tushar'])                # Output: 85
print(scores['Salil'])                 # Output: 92
print(scores['Mayukh'])                # Output: 99
```

DataFrames

A DataFrame is a two-dimensional labeled data structure that is similar to a table in a relational database or a spreadsheet. It consists of rows and columns, where each column can contain different data types. DataFrames are highly efficient for handling and analyzing structured data.

To create a DataFrame, we can use the 'pd.DataFrame()' function in Pandas.

```python
import pandas as pd

# Create a DataFrame of siblings' information
data = {'Name': ['Nibedita', 'Tushar', 'Salil', 'Mayukh',
'Bidisha'],
        'Age': [20, 18, 23, 26, 20],
        'Hobby': ['Problem Solving', 'Gaming', 'Gaining New
Insights', 'Programming', 'Sleeping']}

df = pd.DataFrame(data)
```

In the code snippet above, we imported the Pandas library and created a DataFrame called 'df' using a dictionary 'data'. The keys of the dictionary represent column names, and the values represent the corresponding column values. By default, the index labels are assigned as integers starting from 0. We can access columns in a DataFrame using their names.

```python
# Accessing columns in a DataFrame
print(df['Name'])       # Output: ['Nibedita', 'Tushar', 'Salil',
'Mayukh', 'Bidisha']
print(df['Age'])        # Output: [20, 18, 23, 26, 20]
print(df['Hobby'])      # Output: ['Problem Solving',
'Gaming', 'Gaining New Insights', 'Programming', 'Sleeping']
```

Or if you want them to come as a table, then you can print it directly too.

```
print(df)

# Output:
     Name  Age          Hobby
0  Nibedita  20      Problem Solving
1   Tushar  18            Gaming
2    Salil  23  Gaining New Insights
3   Mayukh  26         Programming
4  Bidisha  20           Sleeping
```

We can also access specific rows in a DataFrame using the 'iloc' or 'loc' attributes.

```
# Accessing rows in a DataFrame using iloc
print(df.iloc[0])

# Output:
Name          Nibedita
Age                 20
Hobby    Problem Solving
Name: 0, dtype: object


# Accessing rows in a DataFrame using loc
print(df.loc[4])

# Output:
Name      Bidisha
Age            20
```

```
Hobby    Sleeping
Name: 4, dtype: object
```

Data Manipulation with Series and DataFrames

Pandas provides a wide range of functions and methods to manipulate and transform data in Series and DataFrames. Let's explore some commonly used operations.

1. Filtering Data:

We can filter data in Series and DataFrames based on specific conditions. For example, to filter 'siblings' who have an age greater than 18 in our DataFrame 'df':

```
# Filtering data in a DataFrame
filtered_data = df[df['Age'] > 18]
```

2. Adding and Removing Columns:

We can add new columns or remove existing columns in a DataFrame. For example, to add a new column called 'menu_chicken' to our DataFrame 'df':

```
# Adding a new column to a DataFrame
df['menu_chicken'] = ['Chicken Pakoda', 'Chicken Roll',
'Chicken Fry', 'Chicken Biryani', 'Butter Chicken']
```

- ***To remove a column, we can use the 'drop()'
  method:***

```
# Removing a column from a DataFrame
df = df.drop('menu_chicken', axis=1)
```

3. Aggregating Data:

Pandas provides functions to perform various aggregation operations on Series and DataFrames. For example, to calculate the mean age of the siblings in our DataFrame 'df':

```
# Aggregating data in a DataFrame
mean_age = df['Age'].mean()
```

After mastering the concepts of Series and DataFrames in Pandas, there are a few additional points that the Python programmers should be aware of to enhance their data manipulation skills. Let's explore these concepts along with relevant code snippets.

4. Handling Missing Data:

Real-world datasets often have missing values. Pandas provides functions to handle missing data efficiently. For example, to check for missing values in a DataFrame.

```
# Checking for missing values
print(df.isnull())
To drop rows or columns containing missing values:

# Dropping rows with missing values
df = df.dropna()
```

```
# Dropping columns with missing values
df = df.dropna(axis=1)
```

- To fill missing values with a specific value:

```
# Filling missing values with a specific value
df = df.fillna(0)
```

5. Data Sorting:

Pandas allows sorting data based on column values. For
example, to sort a DataFrame by the 'Age' column in
ascending order:

```
# Sorting a DataFrame by a column
df = df.sort_values('Age')
```

* To sort a DataFrame by multiple columns:

```
# Sorting a DataFrame by multiple columns
df = df.sort_values(['Hobby', 'Age'])
```

6. Grouping and Aggregating Data:

Grouping data based on specific columns and performing
aggregate operations is a common task in data analysis.
Pandas provides the 'groupby()' function for this purpose. For

example, to calculate the 'mean age' for each 'hobby' in our DataFrame 'df':

```
# Grouping and aggregating data
mean_age_by_hobby = df.groupby('Hobby')['Age'].mean()
```

7. Merging DataFrames:

In real-world scenarios, we often need to combine multiple DataFrames based on common columns. Pandas provides the 'merge()' function for merging DataFrames. For example, if we have two DataFrames, 'df1' and 'df2', with a common column 'ID', we can merge them.

```
# Merging DataFrames
merged_df = pd.merge(df1, df2, on='ID')
```

8. Applying Functions to Data:

Pandas allows applying custom functions to Series and DataFrames. For example, to apply a function to a column in a DataFrame and create a new column based on the result:

```
# Applying a function to a column
df['New_Column'] = df['Age'].apply(lambda x: x + 1)
```

9. Data Visualization:

Pandas integrates well with popular data visualization libraries such as Matplotlib and Seaborn, enabling us to create insightful plots and charts. For example, to create a histogram of the 'Age' column in our DataFrame 'df':

```python
import matplotlib.pyplot as plt

# Creating a histogram
plt.hist(df['Age'])
plt.xlabel('Age')
plt.ylabel('Frequency')
plt.title('Age Distribution')
plt.show()
```

Output:

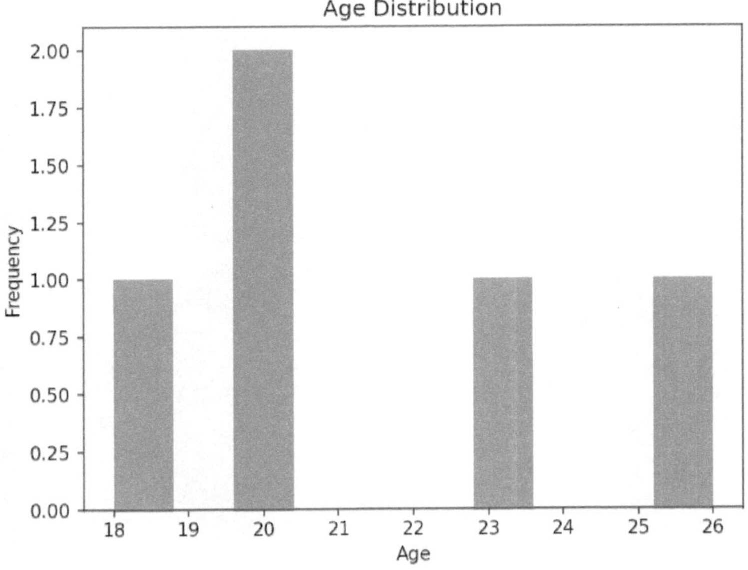

By mastering these additional concepts, Python programmers can elevate their data manipulation skills using Pandas and effectively analyze and visualize data in various real-world scenarios.

Remember, practice is key to mastering these concepts. Exploring the Pandas documentation and working on hands-on projects will further enhance your understanding and proficiency in data manipulation with Series and DataFrames.

4. File Handling:

4.1. Reading and writing files

4.2. CSV and JSON file formats

4.1. Reading and writing files

File handling is a fundamental aspect of programming, enabling developers to interact with data stored in files on a computer's filesystem. In Python, file handling is remarkably straightforward and offers a plethora of tools to read and write data efficiently.

In this section, you will gain an in-depth exploration of file handling in Python. We'll be focusing on reading and writing files and offering practical code snippets to illustrate key concepts.

Understanding File Modes

Before delving into reading and writing files, it's crucial to comprehend file modes. File modes in Python are represented by strings that determine how a file should be opened and what operations are allowed. Here are the most commonly used file modes:

- 'r': Read mode (default). It allows reading data from an existing file.
- 'w': Write mode. It creates a new file or overwrites the existing file. Be cautious as it will erase the file's content.

- 'a': Append mode. It creates a new file if it doesn't exist or appends data to an existing file.
- 'x': Exclusive creation mode. It creates a new file, but if the file already exists, the operation will fail.
- 'b': Binary mode. It's used with other modes like 'rb' or 'wb' to handle binary data (images, audio, etc.).
- 't': Text mode (default). It's used with other modes like 'rt' or 'wt' to handle text data.

Let's dive into reading and writing files with Python!

Reading Files:

To read files in Python, we use the built-in function 'open()', which takes the file name and the mode as its arguments. The 'open()' function returns a file object that allows us to interact with the file's content. It's essential to close the file using the 'close()' method when you're done reading to release system resources.

```python
# Open the file in read mode
file_name = "sample.txt"
with open(file_name, 'r') as file:
    content = file.read()
    print(content)
```

```python
"""
It'll read the entire content of the file and the file will be
automatically closed after leaving the 'with' block
"""
```

In this example, we open the file "sample.txt" in read mode
('r') using the 'open()' function. The 'with' statement ensures
that the file is automatically closed when the block is exited.

Reading Line by Line:

Sometimes, reading the entire content of a file into memory
might not be feasible for large files. Instead, we can read the
file line by line using the 'readline()' method or use a loop to
iterate through the file object.

```python
# Open the file in read mode
file_name = "sample.txt"
with open(file_name, 'r') as file:
    for line in file:
        print(line.strip())


"""
It'll read and print the content line by line and we can use
strip()
to remove extra newline characters.
"""
```

Writing Files:

Writing files in Python is also accomplished with the 'open()' function, but this time we use the write mode ('w') or append mode ('a'). We need to be cautious when using write mode as it will erase the existing content of the file. To avoid accidental data loss, we consider using append mode.

```python
# Open the file in write mode
file_name = "output.txt"
with open(file_name, 'w') as file:
    file.write("Hello, this is a sample text.\n")
    file.write("Writing data to a file is easy!\n")


# It'll write data to the file.
```

In this code, we open the file "output.txt" in write mode ('w') and use the 'write()' method to add data to the file. Note the use of the newline character ("\n") to start a new line after each write.

Appending to Files:

To append data to an existing file, use the append mode ('a') instead of write mode ('w'). This ensures that the existing content is preserved, and new data is added to the end of the file.

```python
# Open the file in append mode
file_name = "output.txt"
with open(file_name, 'a') as file:
```

```python
    file.write("This data is appended to the
file.\n")

# It'll append data to the file.
```

Handling Exceptions:

When working with files, there's always a possibility of errors, such as the file not existing, not having appropriate permissions, or running out of disk space. To handle such situations gracefully, we can use exception handling with the 'try-except' block.

```python
file_name = "non_existent_file.txt"
try:
    with open(file_name, 'r') as file:
        content = file.read()
        print(content)
except FileNotFoundError:
    print(f"The file '{file_name}' does not exist.")
except PermissionError:
    print(f"You don't have permission to read '{file_name}'.")
except Exception as e:
    print(f"An error occurred: {str(e)}")
```

Working with Binary Files:

Binary files, such as images, audio files, or binary data, require a different approach from regular text files. For binary file handling, we use the binary mode ('b') in conjunction with the read ('rb') or write ('wb') mode.

```python
# Reading a binary file (image) and writing it to another file
input_file = "input_image.png"
output_file = "output_image.png"

with open(input_file, 'rb') as file_in:
    with open(output_file, 'wb') as file_out:
        content = file_in.read()
        file_out.write(content)
```

In this example, we read the content of the binary file "input_image.png" in read binary mode ('rb') and write the same content to "output_image.png" using write binary mode ('wb').

Additional Points on Reading and Writing Files in Python:

1. Reading and Writing Text Files with Encoding:

When dealing with text files that are not in the default encoding (UTF-8), you can specify the encoding explicitly using the 'encoding' parameter.

```python
file_name = "non_utf8_file.txt"
with open(file_name, 'r', encoding='latin-1') as file:
    content = file.read()
```

2. _Reading Lines into a List:_

You can read all the lines of a file into a list using the 'readlines()' method. This is useful when you need to process each line separately.

```python
file_name = "data.txt"
with open(file_name, 'r') as file:
    lines = file.readlines()
```

3. _Writing a List to a File:_

If you have data in a list and want to write each element as a separate line in a file, you can use the 'writelines()' method.

```python
data = ["Line 1", "Line 2", "Line 3"]
with open("output.txt", 'w') as file:
    file.writelines(data)
```

4. _Using 'seek()' and 'tell()' for File Pointer Manipulation:_

The 'seek()' method allows you to move the file pointer to a specific location in the file, and 'tell()' returns the current position of the file pointer.

```python
with open("data.txt", 'r') as file:
    print(file.tell())      # Print current file pointer position
    file.seek(5)            # Move the file pointer to the 6th byte
    content = file.read()
```

5. Contextlib for File Handling:

You can use the 'contextlib' module to create custom context managers for file handling, offering more control over file operations.

```python
from contextlib import contextmanager

@contextmanager
def file_opener(file_name, mode):
    file = open(file_name, mode)
    yield file
    file.close()


# Usage
with file_opener("data.txt", "r") as file:
    content = file.read()
```

6. Handling Large Files Efficiently:

For large files, reading the entire content into memory may not be practical. Instead, you can process the file in smaller chunks using a loop.

```python
with open("large_file.txt", "r") as file:
    chunk_size = 1024              # Process 1KB at a time
    while True:
        chunk = file.read(chunk_size)
        if not chunk:
            break

        # Process the chunk
```

Remember, always close files after working with them to avoid potential issues with file locks and resource management. The 'with' statement ensures proper file closure, but if you opt for the traditional approach, make sure to call the 'close()' method explicitly.

Understanding file handling in Python is a valuable skill for any programmer. Whether you're working with small text files or large datasets, Python's file handling capabilities provide an array of tools to handle various scenarios efficiently. By mastering these techniques, you can effectively read and write data to and from files, making your applications more versatile and robust.

4.2. CSV AND JSON FILE FORMATS

File handling is a fundamental aspect of programming that allows us to read and write data from and to files. It plays a crucial role in handling various types of data, and two popular file formats for storing structured data are CSV (Comma Separated Values) and JSON (JavaScript Object Notation). Both formats have their own strengths and use cases, making them essential tools in data processing, storage, and exchange. In this article, we will explore CSV and JSON file formats, their differences, advantages, and how to work with them in Python.

1. Understanding CSV (Comma Separated Values)

CSV is a simple and widely used file format for storing tabular data. It represents data in a plain-text form, where each line of the file typically corresponds to a row, and values within the row are separated by commas or other delimiters like tabs or semicolons. CSV files can be easily created and edited using common spreadsheet applications like Microsoft Excel or Google Sheets.

<u>**Advantages of CSV:**</u>

- ***Simplicity:*** CSV files have a straightforward structure, making them easy to create, read, and modify manually or programmatically.
- ***Compatibility:*** CSV files can be imported and exported by a wide range of software applications, making them highly interoperable.
- ***Lightweight:*** CSV files do not consume much disk space, making them suitable for large datasets.

<u>**Working with CSV in Python:**</u>

Python provides a built-in module called 'csv' to handle CSV files effortlessly. Let's explore some common operations using this module.

```
Reading Data from a CSV File:
import csv

# Open the CSV file in read mode
with open('data.csv', 'r') as file:
    reader = csv.reader(file)

    # Iterate through each row in the CSV file
    for row in reader:
        # Process the data in each row (row is a list of values)
        print(row)
```

```python
import csv

data = [
    ['Name', 'Age', 'Passion'],
    ['Nibedita', 20, 'Programmer'],
    ['Bidisha', 21, 'Blogger'],
    ['Nibe', 22, 'Graphic-Designer']
]


# Open the CSV file in write mode
with open('output.csv', 'w', newline='') as file:
    writer = csv.writer(file)

    # Write data to the CSV file row by row
    for row in data:
        writer.writerow(row)
```

2. Understanding JSON (JavaScript Object Notation)

JSON is a lightweight and human-readable data interchange format. It is primarily used for transmitting data between a server and a web application as an alternative to XML. JSON data is represented in key-value pairs and follows a hierarchical structure. Data in JSON format is often stored in a nested manner, making it highly suitable for complex and unstructured data.

Advantages of JSON:

- *Flexibility:* JSON can handle nested and complex data structures, allowing it to represent data in a more flexible way compared to CSV.
- *Readability:* JSON is easy for both humans and machines to read and understand, making it an ideal choice for data transmission.
- *Language Independence:* JSON data can be processed in various programming languages due to its simplicity and standardization.

Working with JSON in Python:

Python provides a built-in module called 'json' to work with JSON data effectively. Let's explore some common operations using this module.

Reading Data from a JSON File:

```python
import json

# Open the JSON file in read mode
with open('data.json', 'r') as file:
    data = json.load(file)

# 'data' now contains the JSON data as a Python dictionary
or list
print(data)
Writing Data to a JSON File:
```

```python
import json

data = {
    'name': 'Nibedita Sahu',
    'age': 20,
    'region': 'India'
}

# Open the JSON file in write mode
with open('output.json', 'w') as file:
    json.dump(data, file)
```

3. Differences between CSV and JSON

While both CSV and JSON are used for storing data, they have some fundamental differences that make them suitable for different use cases.

Data Representation:

- CSV represents data as flat tables, with each row corresponding to a record, and each column representing a field.
- JSON represents data in a hierarchical and nested manner, making it more flexible for complex data structures.

Data Types:

- CSV is limited in terms of data types.

All values are treated as strings, and there is no native way to represent complex data structures like nested dictionaries or lists.

- JSON supports a wider range of data types, including strings, numbers, booleans, arrays, and nested objects, making it more versatile for representing structured and unstructured data.

Ease of Reading:

- CSV files are generally easier for humans to read and understand due to their flat structure and simple representation.
- JSON, while still human-readable, can become more complex and harder to interpret when dealing with deeply nested data.

Use Cases:

- CSV is well-suited for simple tabular data, such as spreadsheets, logs, and database exports.
- JSON is ideal for storing and exchanging complex data structures, such as configurations, API responses, and data transmitted between web applications and servers.

4. Choosing Between CSV and JSON

The choice between CSV and JSON largely depends on the nature of the data you need to work with and the use case you are addressing.

Use CSV When:

- Dealing with simple tabular data like spreadsheets or databases.
- The data is relatively flat and does not require nested or complex structures.
- You need a lightweight and straightforward format for data storage.

Use JSON When:

- Working with complex and hierarchical data structures.
- Data needs to be exchanged between web applications and APIs.
- The data contains nested objects or arrays that need to be preserved.

5. Tips for Efficient File Handling

Regardless of whether you choose CSV or JSON, consider these tips for efficient file handling in Python:

- **Context Managers:** Always use context managers (with statement) when working with files in Python. It ensures that the file is properly closed after use, even if an error occurs during the execution.

- ***Batch Processing:*** When dealing with large datasets, consider processing the data in batches to avoid memory overflow.
- ***Error Handling:*** Implement proper error handling when reading or writing files to handle situations like missing files, file permissions, or unexpected data.
- ***Data Validation:*** Validate data before writing to a file to ensure data integrity and avoid issues with the file's structure.
- ***File Formats and Extensions:*** While file extensions are not essential for file handling in Python, using appropriate extensions like ".csv" for CSV files and ".json" for JSON files helps in clear identification and organization.

CSV and JSON are both valuable file formats for handling structured data in Python. While CSV is suitable for tabular data with a simple structure, JSON shines when dealing with complex and nested data. Understanding the differences between these formats and their respective advantages can help you make informed decisions when it comes to storing, processing, and exchanging data in your Python applications. Always remember to follow best practices for efficient file handling and ensure data integrity to create robust and reliable programs.

5. String Manipulation:

5.1. String operations

5.2. Regular expressions

5.1. STRING OPERATIONS

String manipulation is a fundamental concept in programming, and Python offers a rich set of tools for working with strings. Strings in Python are sequences of characters, and they play a crucial role in various applications, such as text processing, data parsing, and user interaction. In this article, we will explore some of the most common and useful string operations in Python.

1. Concatenation

Concatenation is the process of combining two or more strings into a single string. In Python, you can use the '+' operator to concatenate strings.

```
name1 = "Nibedita"
name2 = "Bidisha"
full_name = name1 + " " + name2
print(full_name)          # Output: Nibedita Bidisha
```

2. String Length

To find the length of a string, you can use the built-in 'len()' function. It returns the number of characters in the string, including spaces.

```
name = "Bidisha"
length = len(name)
print(length)        # Output: 7
```

3. _String Indexing_

String indexing is used to access individual characters in a string. In Python, strings are zero-indexed, meaning the first character has an index of 0, the second character has an index of 1, and so on.

```python
name = "Tushar"
first_character = name[0]
print(first_character)        # Output: T


third_character = name[2]
print(third_character)        # Output: s
```

4. _Slicing_

Slicing allows you to extract a portion of a string. It is done using the colon ':' operator. The syntax for slicing is 'string[start:stop]', where 'start' is the index of the first character to include, and 'stop' is the index of the first character to exclude.

```python
name = "Salil"
partial_name = name[2:5]
print(partial_name)        # Output: lil
Or if you can do:


name = "Mayukh"
partial_name = name[1:-2]
print(partial_name)        # Output: ayu
```

If you omit the 'start' index, Python assumes it as 0. Similarly, if you omit the 'stop' index, Python considers it as the length of the string.

```
name = "Nibedita"
first_three_chars = name[:4]
print(first_three_chars)        # Output: Nibe

last_two_chars = name[-4:]
print(last_two_chars)           # Output: dita
```

5. String Methods

Python provides a plethora of built-in string methods that make string manipulation a breeze. Some commonly used methods:

5.1. lower() and upper():

These methods return a new string with all characters converted to lowercase or uppercase, respectively.

```
text = "Hello, World!"
lowercase_text = text.lower()
print(lowercase_text)           # Output: hello, world!

uppercase_text = text.upper()
print(uppercase_text)           # Output: HELLO, WORLD!
```

5.2. strip(), lstrip(), and rstrip():

'strip()' removes leading and trailing whitespace characters from the string. 'lstrip()' removes leading whitespace, and 'rstrip()' removes trailing whitespace.

```python
string_with_spaces = "   Hello, Python!   "
stripped_string = string_with_spaces.strip()
print(stripped_string)              # Output: Hello, Python!
```

5.3. split():

The 'split()' method splits a string into a list of substrings based on a specified delimiter. By default, it splits the string at spaces.

```python
sentence = "Python is an amazing language"
words = sentence.split()
print(words)     # Output: ['Python', 'is', 'an', 'amazing',
'language']
```

You can also provide a custom delimiter as an argument to 'split()'.

```python
date = "2023-07-31"
day_month_year = date.split("-")
print(day_month_year)  # Output: ['2023', '07', '31']
```

5.4. join():

The 'join()' method is used to join elements of an iterable (e.g., a list) into a single string using the specified separator.

```python
words = ['Python', 'is', 'awesome']
joined_string = " ".join(words)
print(joined_string)  # Output: Python is awesome
```

5.5. replace():

The 'replace()' method replaces all occurrences of a
substring with another substring.

```python
text = "Hello, Nibedita!"
modified_text = text.replace("Nibedita", "NS")
print(modified_text)          # Output: Hello, NS!
```

5.6. startswith() and endswith():

These methods check if a string starts or ends with a
given substring and return a boolean value.

```python
name = "Nibedita"
starts_with_n = name.startswith("N")
print(starts_with_n)     # Output: True

ends_with_a = name.endswith("a")
print(ends_with_a)       # Output: True
```

6. Formatting Strings

Python provides different ways to format strings effectively.
Here are two common methods:

6.1. f-strings (formatted strings):

F-strings are a convenient way to embed expressions inside string literals for formatting.

```python
name = "Tushar"
age = 18
formatted_string = f"My name is {name} and I am {age} years old."
print(formatted_string)

# Output: My name is Tushar and I am 18 years old.
```

6.2. format():

The 'format()' method allows you to insert values into placeholders within a string.

```python
name = "Salil"
age = 22
formatted_string = "My name is {} and I am {} years old.".format(name, age)
print(formatted_string)

# Output: My name is Salil and I am 22 years old.
```

You can also use indexing in placeholders to specify the order of variables in the 'format()' method.

```python
name = "Mayukh"
age = 25
formatted_string = "My name is {1} and I am {0} years old.".format(age, name)
```

```
print(formatted_string)

# Output: My name is Mayukh and I am 25 years old.
```

7. String Validation

Python provides several methods to validate strings, such as checking if a string contains only alphanumeric characters, digits, alphabets, etc.

7.1. isalpha():

The 'isalpha()' method returns 'True' if all characters in the string are alphabets; otherwise, it returns 'False'.

```
text1 = "PythonIsFun"
is_alpha = text1.isalpha()
print(is_alpha)          # Output: True


# But if you will write a sentence:
text2 = "Python is fun"
is_alpha = text2.isalpha()
print(is_alpha)          # Output: False
```

7.2. isdigit():

The 'isdigit()' method returns 'True' if all characters in the string are digits; otherwise, it returns 'False'.

```
phone_number = "1234567890"
is_digit = phone_number.isdigit()
print(is_digit)          # Output: True
```

7.3. *isalnum()*:

The 'isalnum()' method returns 'True' if all characters in the string are alphanumeric; otherwise, it returns 'False'.

```python
username = "NibeditaSahu2023"
is_alphanumeric = username.isalnum()
print(is_alphanumeric)       # Output: True
```

In this section, we explored various string operations in Python for string manipulation. We covered concatenation, string length, string indexing, slicing, commonly used string methods, formatting strings, and string validation. By leveraging these string operations, you can perform powerful text processing and data manipulation tasks in Python.

Understanding string manipulation is essential for any Python programmer, as it forms the basis for many real-world applications. Whether you're working with user inputs, reading files, or dealing with APIs, having a good grasp of string operations will undoubtedly make your code more efficient and robust. So, keep practicing and exploring the possibilities of string manipulation in Python!

5.2. Regular expressions

Regular expressions, often referred to as "regex" or "regexp," are powerful tools for pattern matching and text manipulation in Python and many other programming languages. They allow you to search for specific patterns in strings and perform various operations based on those patterns. Python provides the re module, which supports regular expressions.

Here's a definition of regular expressions in Python:

Regular expressions in Python are a sequence of characters that define a search pattern. They can be used to find, match, and manipulate strings based on specific patterns, making text processing and data extraction more efficient and flexible.

To use regular expressions in Python, you need to import the re module.

Here are some common functions and methods provided by the re module in Python:

1. re.match():

Determine if the regular expression matches at the beginning of the string.

```python
import re

pattern = r'^Hello'
text = 'Hello, World!'

match = re.match(pattern, text)

if match:
    print('Pattern matched at the beginning.')
else:
    print('Pattern not found at the beginning.')
```

2. re.search():

Search for the first occurrence of a pattern in the entire string.

```python
import re

pattern = r'World'
text = 'Hello, World!'

search_result = re.search(pattern, text)

if search_result:
    print('Pattern found at index:', search_result.start())
else:
    print('Pattern not found.')
```

3. _re.findall()_:

Find all occurrences of a pattern in the string and return them
as a list.

```
import re

pattern = r'\d+'  # Matches one or more digits
text = 'There are 7 cats and 12 dogs in the neighborhood.'

matches = re.findall(pattern, text)

print('Found digits:', matches)
```

4. _re.sub()_:

Replace all occurrences of a pattern in the string with a given
replacement.

```
import re

pattern = r'\bapple\b'
text = 'I have an apple, and she has an apple too.'

replacement = 'orange'
new_text = re.sub(pattern, replacement, text)

print('Original text:', text)
print('Modified text:', new_text)
```

5. _re.split()_:

Split the string by occurrences of the pattern.

```python
import re

pattern = r'\s+'  # Matches one or more whitespace characters
text = 'Hello    World  \t of\tPython'

words = re.split(pattern, text)

print('Split words:', words)
```

These are just some of the basic operations that regular expressions can perform in Python. Regular expressions provide a rich set of features and syntax for more complex pattern matching and manipulation tasks. They are incredibly helpful when dealing with text data and can save a lot of time and effort in data processing and analysis.

6. Object-Oriented Programming (OOP):

6.1. Classes and objects

6.2. Inheritance and polymorphism

6.3. Advanced OOP concepts

6.1. Classes and Objects

In Python, a class is a blueprint or template that defines the structure and behaviour of objects. An object, on the other hand, is an instance of a class, created based on that blueprint. Classes and objects are fundamental concepts in object-oriented programming (OOP), which allows us to model real-world entities, encapsulate data, and provide functionalities.

Defining a Class:

To create a class in Python, you use the class keyword, followed by the class name and a colon. Inside the class, you define attributes and methods that describe the characteristics and actions of the objects created from the class.

```python
class Car:
    # Class attributes
    brand = "Toyota"
    year = 2023

    # Class methods
    def start_engine(self):
        return f"{self.brand}'s engine started!"

    def accelerate(self, speed):
        return f"{self.brand}'s accelerating to {speed} km/h"
```

In this example, we defined a class called Car. It has two class attributes (brand and year) and two class methods (start_engine() and accelerate()).

Creating Objects:

Once you have a class, you can create instances (objects) of that class. To do this, you call the class as if it were a function, which creates a new object based on the class blueprint.

```python
# Creating two Car objects
nibedita_car = Car()
bidisha_car = Car()
```

In this example, we created two objects nibedita_car and bidisha_car from the Car class.

Accessing Attributes and Methods:

You can access the attributes and methods of an object using the dot notation.

```python
print(nibedita_car.brand)      # Output: Toyota
print(bidisha_car.year)        # Output: 2023
print(nibedita_car.start_engine())
# Output: Toyota's engine started!

print(bidisha_car.accelerate(80))
# Output: Toyota's accelerating to 80 km/h
```

Constructor (__init__ method):

The __init__ method is a special method that gets called automatically when an object is created. It is used to initialize object-specific attributes.

```python
class Person:
    def __init__(self, name, age):
        self.name = name
        self.age = age

    def say_hello(self):
        return f"Hello, my name is {self.name} and I am {self.age} years old."

tushar = Person("Tushar", 18)
salil = Person("Salil", 22)
mayukh = Person("Mayukh", 25)

print(tushar.say_hello())
# Output: Hello, my name is Tushar and I am 18 years old.

print(salil.say_hello())
# Output: Hello, my name is Salil and I am 22 years old.

print(mayukh.say_hello())
# Output: Hello, my name is Mayukh and I am 25 years old.
```

Instance vs. Class Attributes:

Instance attributes are specific to each object and can be different for different instances.

Class attributes, on the other hand, are shared among all instances of the class.

```python
class Dog:
    species = "Canine"  # Class attribute

    def __init__(self, name):
        self.name = name  # Instance attribute

tommy_dog = Dog("Tommy")
print(tommy_dog.name)    # Output: Tommy

print(tommy_dog.species)
# Output: Canine (shared among all instances)
```

In summary, classes and objects are essential in Python's object-oriented programming paradigm. Classes serve as blueprints for creating objects, and objects are instances of those classes with their own unique characteristics and behaviors. They enable code organization, encapsulation, and reusability, making it easier to manage complex applications.

6.2. Inheritance and Polymorphism

Inheritance:

Inheritance is a fundamental concept in object-oriented programming that allows a class (called the subclass or derived class) to inherit properties and behaviors from another class (called the superclass or base class). The subclass can reuse the attributes and methods of the superclass and can also have its own specific attributes and methods.

Defining a Base Class:

To create a base class, you define a regular class with its attributes and methods. The subclass can then inherit from this base class using the class SubClassName(BaseClassName):

```python
class Animal:
    def __init__(self, name):
        self.name = name

    def make_sound(self):
        return "Some generic sound"

    def move(self):
        return "Some generic movement"
```

In this example, we have a base class Animal with attributes name, and methods make_sound() and move().

Defining a Subclass:

To create a subclass that inherits from the base class, simply pass the base class name in parentheses when defining the subclass.

```python
class Dog(Animal):
    def __init__(self, name, breed):
        super().__init__(name)
        self.breed = breed

    def make_sound(self):
        return "Woof!"

    def move(self):
        return "Run like a dog"
```

Here, we created a subclass Dog that inherits from the Animal base class. The super() function is used to call the constructor of the base class and initialize the name attribute. The subclass also overrides the make_sound() and move() methods.

Using Inheritance:

Now, we can create objects of the subclass Dog and access the attributes and methods from both the subclass and the base class.

```
dog = Dog("Buddy", "Golden Retriever")
print(dog.name)        # Output: Buddy
print(dog.breed)       # Output: Golden Retriever
print(dog.make_sound()) # Output: Woof!
print(dog.move())      # Output: Run like a dog
```

As you can see, the Dog subclass has access to the name attribute and the methods make_sound() and move() from the Animal base class.

Polymorphism:

Polymorphism is another key concept in object-oriented programming, which allows objects of different classes to be treated as objects of a common superclass. It enables a single interface to represent multiple types, providing flexibility and code reusability.

```
def animal_sound(animal):
    return animal.make_sound()


# Creating instances of both the base class and the subclass
cat = Animal("Whiskers")
dog = Dog("Buddy", "Golden Retriever")
```

```
print(animal_sound(cat))  # Output: Some generic sound
print(animal_sound(dog))  # Output: Woof!
```

In this example, we created a function animal_sound() that
takes an object as an argument. Both Animal and Dog classes
have a make_sound() method, so we can pass objects of both
classes to the animal_sound() function. This demonstrates
polymorphism, as the same method call behaves differently
based on the type of the object passed.

Inheritance and polymorphism are powerful concepts in
object-oriented programming that facilitate code
organization, reusability, and flexibility. Inheritance allows
subclasses to inherit attributes and methods from a base
class, enabling code reuse and specialization. Polymorphism,
on the other hand, allows different objects to be treated
uniformly based on their common interface, providing a
flexible and consistent programming approach. Together,
these concepts make Python an expressive and efficient
language for building complex and maintainable applications.

6.3. ADVANCED OOP CONCEPTS

Python is a versatile language that supports advanced Object-Oriented Programming (OOP) concepts. In addition to basic OOP principles like classes, objects, inheritance, and polymorphism, Python also provides advanced features that enhance code modularity, reusability, and maintainability. Let's explore some of these advanced OOP concepts with code snippets:

1. Encapsulation:

Encapsulation is the concept of hiding the implementation details of an object from the outside world. It allows us to protect the internal state of an object and control access to its attributes and methods. Python provides access control using naming conventions:

- _attribute: A single underscore indicates a private attribute.
- __attribute: A double underscore indicates a strongly private attribute (name-mangled).

```python
class BankAccount:
    def __init__(self, account_number, balance):
        self._account_number = account_number
        self.__balance = balance
```

```python
    def deposit(self, amount):
        self.__balance += amount

    def withdraw(self, amount):
        if amount <= self.__balance:
            self.__balance -= amount
        else:
            print("Insufficient balance.")

    def get_balance(self):
        return self.__balance


account = BankAccount("123456789", 1000)
print(account.get_balance())  # Output: 1000

account.withdraw(500)
print(account.get_balance())  # Output: 500

print(account.__balance)
# AttributeError: 'BankAccount' object has no attribute
'__balance'
```

In this example, we use a double underscore to make the
__balance attribute private. Attempting to access it directly
will raise an AttributeError.

2. Property Decorators:

Python's property decorator allows us to create getter, setter, and deleter methods for class attributes. This helps in controlling attribute access and validation.

```python
class Rectangle:
    def __init__(self, width, height):
        self._width = width
        self._height = height

    @property
    def width(self):
        return self._width

    @width.setter
    def width(self, value):
        if value > 0:
            self._width = value
        else:
            raise ValueError("Width must be greater than 0.")

    @property
    def height(self):
        return self._height

    @height.setter
    def height(self, value):
        if value > 0:
            self._height = value
        else:
            raise ValueError("Height must be greater than 0.")

    def area(self):
```

```python
        return self._width * self._height


rect = Rectangle(5, 3)
print(rect.area())    # Output: 15

rect.width = 10
rect.height = 6
print(rect.area())    # Output: 60

rect.width = -2      # Raises ValueError: Width must be
greater than 0.
```

In this example, we use property decorators to create getter and setter methods for the width and height attributes of the Rectangle class.

3. Class Methods and Static Methods:

Python supports class methods and static methods. Class methods take the class as the first argument (usually named cls) and can access or modify class-level attributes. Static methods do not depend on the class or instance and are used for utility functions within the class.

```python
class MathUtils:
    PI = 3.14159
    @classmethod
    def circle_area(cls, radius):
        return cls.PI * radius * radius
```

```python
    @staticmethod
    def add(a, b):
        return a + b


print(MathUtils.circle_area(5))   # Output: 78.53975
print(MathUtils.add(2, 3))        # Output: 5
```

In this example, we define a MathUtils class with a class method circle_area() to calculate the area of a circle and a static method add() to perform addition.

4. Abstract Base Classes (ABCs):

Abstract Base Classes (ABCs) allow us to define abstract methods that must be implemented by the concrete subclasses. ABCs act as a contract for the subclasses, ensuring that they provide the required functionality.

```python
from abc import ABC, abstractmethod
class Shape(ABC):
    @abstractmethod
    def area(self):
        pass
class Square(Shape):
    def __init__(self, side):
        self.side = side

    def area(self):
        return self.side ** 2
```

```python
class Circle(Shape):
    def __init__(self, radius):
        self.radius = radius

    def area(self):
        return 3.14159 * self.radius ** 2

square = Square(4)
circle = Circle(3)
print(square.area())   # Output: 16
print(circle.area())   # Output: 28.27431
```

In this example, the Shape class is an abstract base class with an abstract method area(). The Square and Circle subclasses implement the area() method, making them concrete subclasses.

Advanced OOP concepts in Python, such as encapsulation, property decorators, class methods, static methods, and abstract base classes, enhance the language's capabilities and promote code modularity, reusability, and maintainability. By leveraging these features, developers can create more sophisticated and efficient object-oriented applications in Python.

7. Modules and Packages:

7.1. Creating and importing modules

7.2. Working with packages

7.1. CREATING AND IMPORTING MODULES

Modules in Python are separate files that contain Python code, including variables, functions, and classes. They allow you to organize your code logically and promote code reusability. Python's module system makes it easy to break a large program into smaller, manageable parts.

Creating a Module:

Creating a module in Python is straightforward. Simply write your code in a separate .py file, and that file becomes a module that can be imported into other Python scripts.

```python
# math_operations.py

def add(a, b):
    return a + b

def subtract(a, b):
    return a - b

def multiply(a, b):
    return a * b

def divide(a, b):
    if b == 0:
```

```python
    raise ValueError("Cannot divide by zero.")
    return a / b
```

In this example, we created a module math_operations.py with four functions: add(), subtract(), multiply(), and divide().

Importing a Module:

To use the functions or variables from a module in another script, you need to import the module using the import keyword.

```python
# main.py
import math_operations

result_add = math_operations.add(5, 3)
print("Addition:", result_add)  # Output: Addition: 8

result_multiply = math_operations.multiply(4, 6)
print("Multiplication:", result_multiply)  # Output:
Multiplication: 24
```

In this example, we imported the math_operations module and used its functions add() and multiply() in the main.py script.

Importing Specific Functions:

You can also import specific functions or variables from a module using the from keyword.

```python
# main.py
from math_operations import add, multiply

result_add = add(5, 3)
print("Addition:", result_add)  # Output: Addition: 8

result_multiply = multiply(4, 6)
print("Multiplication:", result_multiply)  # Output:
Multiplication: 24
```

In this example, we imported only the add() and multiply() functions from the math_operations module.

Using Aliases:

You can assign aliases to module names or function names using the as keyword. This can be useful to avoid naming conflicts or to use shorter names.

```python
# main.py
import math_operations as mo

result_add = mo.add(5, 3)
print("Addition:", result_add)  # Output: Addition: 8

result_multiply = mo.multiply(4, 6)
print("Multiplication:", result_multiply)  # Output:
Multiplication: 24
```

In this example, we imported the math_operations module with an alias mo.

Importing All Functions (Not recommended):

You can import all functions from a module using the from module_name import * syntax. However, this is generally not recommended as it can lead to name clashes and reduce code readability.

```
# main.py
from math_operations import *

result_add = add(5, 3)
print("Addition:", result_add)  # Output: Addition: 8

result_multiply = multiply(4, 6)
print("Multiplication:", result_multiply)  # Output:
Multiplication: 24
```

Creating and Importing Packages:

A package is a collection of related modules. It is simply a directory that contains a special file named __init__.py. This file can be empty or can contain initialization code for the package.

To import modules from a package, you use the import statement with the package name and the module name separated by a dot.

Create a directory named my_package, and inside it, create
two files:

- ***my_package/__init__.py:***

```
# my_package/__init__.py (leave it empty)
```

- ***my_package/utils.py:***

```
# my_package/utils.py

def greet(name):
    return f"Hello, {name}!"
```

Now, create a file named main.py in the same directory as
the my_package directory with the following content:

```
# main.py
from my_package import utils

message = utils.greet("Alice")
print(message)  # Output: Hello, Alice!
```

In this example, we created a package named my_package
and imported the greet() function from the utils module
inside that package.

Creating and importing modules and packages in Python is an essential aspect of building modular, organized, and maintainable code. With modules and packages, you can easily break down large programs into smaller components, promote code reuse, and keep your codebase clean and manageable.

7.2. Working with Packages

In Python, a package is a collection of related modules organized in a directory hierarchy. Packages are used to organize code into logical units, allowing for better code management and reusability. Working with packages involves creating packages, importing modules from packages, and understanding how Python handles package initialization.

Creating a Package:

To create a package, you need to create a directory with a special file named __init__.py inside it. This file can be empty or can contain initialization code for the package. The presence of the __init__.py file indicates that the directory is a package.

Let's create a package named my_package with two modules inside it.

```
my_package/
    __init__.py
    module1.py
    module2.py
```

- ***my_package/__init__.py:***

```
# my_package/__init__.py (leave it empty or add
initialization code if required)
```

- ***my_package/module1.py:***

```
# my_package/module1.py

def function1():
    return "Function 1 from module1"
```

- ***my_package/module2.py:***

```
# my_package/module2.py

def function2():
    return "Function 2 from module2"
```

Importing Modules from Packages:

To use modules from a package, you need to import them using the import statement. You can import modules directly from the package or from subpackages.

Let's assume we have a script named main.py in the same directory as the my_package package.

```
# main.py
from my_package import module1, module2
```

```
print(module1.function1())  # Output: Function 1 from
module1
print(module2.function2())  # Output: Function 2 from
module2
```

In this example, we import module1 and module2 from the my_package package and use their functions.

Importing Subpackages:

You can also import modules from subpackages by using the dot notation.

Assuming we have a subpackage named sub_package inside the my_package package with a module named module3.py.

```
my_package/
    __init__.py
    module1.py
    module2.py
    sub_package/
        __init__.py
        module3.py
```

Working with Packages in Python:

In Python, a package is a collection of related modules organized in a directory hierarchy. Packages are used to organize code into logical units, allowing for better code management and reusability. Working with packages involves creating packages, importing modules from packages, and understanding how Python handles package initialization.

Creating a Package:

To create a package, you need to create a directory with a special file named __init__.py inside it. This file can be empty or can contain initialization code for the package. The presence of the __init__.py file indicates that the directory is a package.

Let's create a package named my_package with two modules inside it.

```markdown
Copy code
my_package/
    __init__.py
    module1.py
    module2.py
my_package/__init__.py:
```

```python
Copy code
# my_package/__init__.py (leave it empty or add initialization code if required)
```

- **_my_package/module1.py:_**

```python
```

```
Copy code
# my_package/module1.py

def function1():
    return "Function 1 from module1"
```

- ***my_package/module2.py:***

```python
Copy code
# my_package/module2.py

def function2():
    return "Function 2 from module2"
```

Importing Modules from Packages:

To use modules from a package, you need to import them using the import statement. You can import modules directly from the package or from subpackages.

Let's assume we have a script named main.py in the same directory as the my_package package.

```python
Copy code
# main.py
from my_package import module1, module2

print(module1.function1())  # Output: Function 1 from module1
```

```
print(module2.function2())  # Output: Function 2 from
module2
In this example, we import module1 and module2 from the
my_package package and use their functions.
```

Importing Subpackages:

You can also import modules from subpackages by using the
dot notation.

Assuming we have a subpackage named sub_package inside
the my_package package with a module named module3.py.

```markdown
Copy code
my_package/
    __init__.py
    module1.py
    module2.py
    sub_package/
        __init__.py
        module3.py
```

- ***my_package/sub_package/module3.py:***

```
# my_package/sub_package/module3.py

def function3():
    return "Function 3 from module3"
```

- ***main.py:***

```
# main.py
from my_package import module1, sub_package

print(module1.function1())     # Output: Function 1 from
module1
print(sub_package.module3.function3())  # Output:
Function 3 from module3
```

In this example, we import sub_package from the my_package package and access the function3() from module3 using the dot notation.

Package Initialization:

When a package is imported, Python executes the code in the __init__.py file inside the package directory. This allows you to perform any necessary initialization tasks for the package.

In the my_package/__init__.py file, we can add some initialization code:

```
# my_package/__init__.py

print("Initializing my_package")

# You can define variables or functions that should be
available when the package is imported
my_variable = 42
```

```python
def greet(name):
    return f"Hello, {name}!"
```

Now, when we import the my_package, the initialization code will be executed:

```python
# main.py
import my_package

print(my_package.my_variable)  # Output: 42
print(my_package.greet("Nibe"))  # Output: Hello, Nibe!
```

In this example, the __init__.py file in the my_package package gets executed when the package is imported, and the variables and functions defined in it are available for use.

Working with packages in Python allows you to organize your code into logical units, improve code reusability, and make your projects more maintainable. By creating packages and using the appropriate import statements, you can structure your codebase effectively and take advantage of Python's modularity features.

8. Error Handling and Exceptions:

8.1. Handling errors and exceptions

8.2. Try-except blocks

8.1. HANDLING ERRORS AND EXCEPTIONS

In Python, exceptions are raised when the program encounters errors or unexpected situations during execution. To prevent the program from terminating abruptly, Python provides a mechanism to handle these exceptions gracefully using try, except, else, and finally blocks. This approach is known as "error handling" or "exception handling."

1. *The try and except Block:*

The try block is used to enclose the code that might raise an exception. If an exception occurs inside the try block, the program immediately jumps to the corresponding except block, and the execution continues from there.

```
try:
    x = 10 / 0
except ZeroDivisionError:
    print("Error: Division by zero")
```

In this example, if a ZeroDivisionError occurs (division by zero), the program jumps to the except block, and the error message is printed.

2. Handling Multiple Exceptions:

You can handle multiple exceptions by including multiple except blocks.

```python
try:
    num = int(input("Enter a number: "))
    result = 10 / num
except ValueError:
    print("Invalid input: Please enter a valid number.")
except ZeroDivisionError:
    print("Error: Division by zero.")
```

In this example, we handle both ValueError (when the input is not a valid number) and ZeroDivisionError (when the input is zero).

3. The else Block:

The else block is optional and executed only if no exceptions are raised in the try block. It is useful for adding code that should run when the try block completes successfully.

```python
try:
    num1 = int(input("Enter the first number: "))
    num2 = int(input("Enter the second number: "))
    result = num1 / num2
except ValueError:
    print("Invalid input: Please enter valid numbers.")
except ZeroDivisionError:
    print("Error: Division by zero.")
```

```python
else:
    print(f"The result is: {result}")
```

In this example, if no exceptions are raised, the program will print the result of the division.

4. *The finally Block:*

The finally block is optional and is used to define cleanup actions that should be performed whether an exception is raised or not. It runs regardless of whether an exception occurred or if it was handled.

```python
try:
    file = open("example.txt", "r")
    content = file.read()
except FileNotFoundError:
    print("Error: File not found.")
else:
    print("File content:", content)
finally:
    file.close()


# This will always execute, whether an exception occurred
or not.
```

In this example, the file is closed in the finally block, ensuring that it is closed properly, even if an exception occurs.

5. _Raising Exceptions:_

You can raise exceptions using the raise statement. This can be useful when you want to handle certain situations manually.

```python
def calculate_square_root(number):
    if number < 0:
        raise ValueError("Input must be a non-negative number.")
    return number ** 0.5


try:
    result = calculate_square_root(-9)
except ValueError as ve:
    print(ve)  # Output: Input must be a non-negative number.
```

In this example, we define a function calculate_square_root() that raises a ValueError if the input is negative.

Handling errors and exceptions in Python is essential for writing robust and reliable programs. Using try, except, else, and finally blocks allows you to gracefully handle errors and prevent your program from crashing unexpectedly. By properly managing exceptions, you can improve the user experience and ensure that your code behaves as expected, even in the face of unexpected circumstances.

8.2. Try-except blocks

In Python, a try-except block is a mechanism used for handling exceptions. It allows you to gracefully handle errors and exceptions that might occur during the execution of a code block. The try block contains the code that might raise an exception, and the except block contains the code that should be executed if an exception occurs.

```
try:
    # Code that might raise an exception
except ExceptionType:
    # Code to handle the exception
```

The try block contains the code that may raise an exception.

The except block is executed only if an exception of type ExceptionType (or its subclass) occurs in the try block.

Let's consider an example where we attempt to divide two numbers, and we want to handle the case where the second number is zero, which would result in a ZeroDivisionError.

```
try:
    num1 = int(input("Enter the first number: "))
    num2 = int(input("Enter the second number: "))
    result = num1 / num2
except ZeroDivisionError:
    print("Error: Division by zero.")
```

In this example, if the user enters zero as the second number, a ZeroDivisionError will be raised. The except block will catch the exception, and the message "Error: Division by zero." will be printed.

You can handle multiple exceptions by including multiple except blocks.

```
try:
    # Code that might raise an exception
except ExceptionType1:
    # Code to handle ExceptionType1
except ExceptionType2:
    # Code to handle ExceptionType2
```

- ***Handling Multiple Exceptions:***

```
try:
    num1 = int(input("Enter the first number: "))
    num2 = int(input("Enter the second number: "))
    result = num1 / num2
except ValueError:
    print("Invalid input: Please enter valid numbers.")
except ZeroDivisionError:
    print("Error: Division by zero.")
```

In this example, we handle both ValueError (when the input is not a valid number) and ZeroDivisionError (when the input is zero).

The else Block:

The else block is optional and is executed only if no exceptions are raised in the try block. It is used for adding code that should run when the try block completes successfully.

```python
try:
    num1 = int(input("Enter the first number: "))
    num2 = int(input("Enter the second number: "))
    result = num1 / num2
except ValueError:
    print("Invalid input: Please enter valid numbers.")
except ZeroDivisionError:
    print("Error: Division by zero.")
else:
    print(f"The result is: {result}")
```

In this example, if no exceptions are raised, the program will print the result of the division.

The finally Block:

The finally block is optional and is used to define cleanup actions that should be performed whether an exception is raised or not. It runs regardless of whether an exception occurred or if it was handled.

```python
try:
    file = open("example.txt", "r")
    content = file.read()
except FileNotFoundError:
```

```python
    print("Error: File not found.")
else:
    print("File content:", content)
finally:
    file.close()  # This will always execute, whether an
exception occurred or not.
```

In this example, the file is closed in the finally block, ensuring that it is closed properly, even if an exception occurs.

try-except blocks in Python provide a way to handle exceptions and errors gracefully. By using these blocks, you can anticipate and handle exceptional situations, preventing your program from terminating abruptly and providing a better user experience. They are an essential part of writing reliable and robust code.

9. Functional Programming:

9.1. Lambda functions

9.2. Map, filter, and reduce functions

9.1. LAMBDA FUNCTIONS

Lambda functions, also known as anonymous functions, are a powerful feature in Python that allows you to create small, one-line functions without the need for a formal function definition using the def keyword. These concise functions are commonly used for simple operations or as arguments to higher-order functions that require a function as an input. Lambda functions provide a quick and convenient way to define and use functions on the fly, making Python code more expressive and readable.

```
lambda arguments: expression
```

In this syntax, arguments represent the input parameters of the function, and expression is a single expression that is evaluated and returned as the result of the function. Lambda functions can have any number of arguments, but they must contain only one expression.

The primary advantage of using lambda functions lies in their conciseness and the fact that they can be used inline with other functions or expressions. Instead of defining a full-fledged named function, you can use a lambda function directly where it's needed. This helps avoid cluttering the code with numerous small functions and improves code maintainability.

Let's explore some examples to better understand lambda functions:

```
add = lambda x, y: x + y
result = add(3, 5)  # Result will be 8
```

In this example, we define a lambda function add that takes two arguments x and y and returns their sum. We then call the lambda function with arguments 3 and 5, and it returns 8.

```
numbers = [1, 2, 3, 4, 5]
squared_numbers = list(map(lambda x: x ** 2, numbers))
# squared_numbers will be [1, 4, 9, 16, 25]
```

Here, we use a lambda function with map(), a higher-order function that applies the given function to each element of the numbers list. The lambda function takes one argument x and returns its square.

Although lambda functions offer several benefits, there are some limitations to be aware of:

- **Single Expression:** Lambda functions are limited to a single expression, which means they cannot contain multiple statements or complex logic. For more complex functions, you would need to use regular named functions defined with def.

- ***No Documentation:*** Lambda functions are anonymous, which means they lack a formal name and, as a result, do not have associated docstrings. Properly documenting lambda functions can be challenging, which may affect code readability and maintainability.

- ***Limited Use Cases:*** While lambda functions are handy for simple operations, they may not be ideal for more intricate tasks that require multiple lines of code or require recursion.

- ***Readability Concerns:*** Using overly complex lambda functions can make code harder to read and understand. It's essential to strike a balance between conciseness and readability.

Despite these limitations, lambda functions are an essential tool in a Python programmer's arsenal. They are particularly useful when working with functions that accept other functions as arguments, such as sorting, filtering, or mapping operations. Additionally, they contribute to the functional programming paradigm in Python and can make code more elegant and expressive when used judiciously.

In summary, lambda functions in Python are small, anonymous functions that provide a concise way to define quick operations on the fly. They are best suited for simple tasks and when used in conjunction with higher-order functions. While they have their limitations, mastering lambda functions can enhance your Python coding skills and lead to more elegant and functional code.

9.2. Map, filter, and reduce functions

"Map," "filter," and "reduce" are three built-in higher-order functions in Python that are often used to perform functional programming operations on iterables, such as lists, tuples, and other sequence types. These functions provide a more concise and expressive way to manipulate data and perform computations. Let's define each of these functions:

Map Function:

The map() function applies a specified function to each item of an iterable (e.g., a list) and returns an iterator that yields the results. It takes two arguments: the function to apply and the iterable. The function can be a regular named function or a lambda function.

Syntax:

```
map(function, iterable)
```

Code:

```python
# Define a function to square a number
def square(x):
    return x ** 2
```

```python
# Use map() to apply the square function to each element
of the list
numbers = [1, 2, 3, 4, 5]
squared_numbers = map(square, numbers)
# squared_numbers will be [1, 4, 9, 16, 25]
```

In this example, the map() function applies the square()
function to each element of the numbers list, resulting in a
new iterator that contains the squared values.

Filter Function:

The filter() function applies a specified function to each item
of an iterable and returns an iterator that yields only the
items for which the function returns True. Similar to map(), it
also takes two arguments: the function to apply and the
iterable.

Syntax:

```python
filter(function, iterable)
```

Code:

```python
# Define a function to check if a number is even
def is_even(x):
    return x % 2 == 0


# Use filter() to keep only the even numbers from the list
numbers = [1, 2, 3, 4, 5]
```

```python
even_numbers = filter(is_even, numbers)
# even_numbers will be [2, 4]
```

In this example, the filter() function applies the is_even()
function to each element of the numbers list, returning only
the elements that satisfy the condition of being even.

Reduce Function:

The reduce() function is part of the functools module in
Python's standard library. It applies a specified binary
function to the items of an iterable in a cumulative way from
left to right and returns a single aggregated value. The
function must take two arguments.

Syntax:

```python
reduce(function, iterable[, initializer])
```

Code:

```python
from functools import reduce

# Define a function to add two numbers
def add(x, y):
    return x + y


# Use reduce() to sum all elements in the list
```

```python
numbers = [1, 2, 3, 4, 5]
sum_all = reduce(add, numbers)
# sum_all will be 15 (1 + 2 + 3 + 4 + 5)
```

In this example, the reduce() function applies the add()
function cumulatively to the elements of the numbers list,
resulting in the sum of all the elements.

It's worth noting that in Python 3, reduce() has been moved
from the built-in namespace to the functools module. So, you
need to import it explicitly as shown in the example above.

In conclusion, "map," "filter," and "reduce" are powerful
higher-order functions in Python that allow you to
manipulate and process data in a functional programming
style. They offer a concise and expressive way to perform
operations on iterables, which can lead to more readable and
maintainable code.

10. Iterators and Generators:

10.1. Iteration protocols

10.2. Creating and using generators

10.1. ITERATION PROTOCOLS

Iteration protocols in Python are a set of rules that define how objects can be iterated using the for loop or other looping constructs. These protocols are fundamental to Python's support for iterable objects, allowing them to work seamlessly with various built-in functions and constructs that expect or support iteration. Two primary iteration protocols in Python are the "iterable protocol" and the "iterator protocol."

Iterable Protocol:

The iterable protocol defines the necessary behavior for objects to be considered iterable. An iterable is any object that can produce an iterator when the iter() function is called on it. An iterable must implement the __iter__() method, which should return an iterator object.

The __iter__() method does not need to create a new iterator object on every call. Instead, it should return an iterator object that can traverse the iterable's elements from the beginning to the end. If the iterable itself is its own iterator, it can return self in the __iter__() method, simplifying the implementation.

```python
class MyIterable:
    def __init__(self, data):
        self.data = data

    def __iter__(self):
        return iter(self.data)

my_list = [1, 2, 3, 4, 5]
iterable_object = MyIterable(my_list)

for item in iterable_object:
    print(item)
```

In this example, MyIterable is an iterable class that contains a list of data. When __iter__() is called, it returns an iterator object created using the iter() function applied to the list.

Iterator Protocol:

The iterator protocol defines the necessary behavior for objects to be considered iterators. An iterator is an object that provides a way to traverse a sequence of elements and retrieve them one by one using the next() function. Iterators must implement two methods: __iter__() and __next__().

The __iter__() method should return the iterator object itself. This method allows iterators to be used in contexts where an iterable is expected.

The __next__() method should return the next element in the sequence. If there are no more elements to return, it should raise the StopIteration exception.

```python
class MyIterator:
    def __init__(self, data):
        self.data = data
        self.index = 0

    def __iter__(self):
        return self

    def __next__(self):
        if self.index >= len(self.data):
            raise StopIteration
        value = self.data[self.index]
        self.index += 1
        return value

my_list = [1, 2, 3, 4, 5]
iterator_object = MyIterator(my_list)

for item in iterator_object:
    print(item)
```

In this example, MyIterator is an iterator class that contains a list of data. The __next__() method allows us to retrieve each element one by one, and the StopIteration exception is raised when there are no more elements left to iterate over.

Python's built-in objects, such as lists, tuples, dictionaries, and strings, already implement the iterable protocol. You can create custom iterable and iterator objects to work seamlessly with Python's iteration protocols, enabling you to use them with for loops and other iterable-related constructs. Understanding and implementing these iteration protocols are essential for creating efficient and reusable iterable and iterator classes in Python.

10.2. CREATING AND USING GENERATORS

Generators in Python are a special type of iterable that allow you to produce a sequence of values on-the-fly. They provide an efficient and memory-friendly way to generate large data sets or infinite sequences without storing them in memory all at once. Generators use a special syntax and offer a convenient way to create iterators using functions with the yield keyword.

To define a generator, you create a function that contains one or more yield statements. When the function is called, it returns a generator object. Each time the generator's next() method is called (implicitly or explicitly), the function's execution is resumed from the point of the last yield statement until the next yield statement is encountered. This way, you can lazily produce values without having to compute the entire sequence upfront.

Let's explore how to create and use generators in Python:

Creating a Generator:

To create a generator, use the yield keyword in a function. The function becomes a generator function, and calling it returns a generator object.

```python
def my_generator():
    yield 1
    yield 2
    yield 3

# Create a generator object
gen = my_generator()
```

Using a Generator:

Generators can be used in various ways, but the most common way is to use them in a for loop. The loop will automatically call the generator's next() method to retrieve the next value until the generator is exhausted (no more yield statements).

```python
# Using the generator in a for loop
for item in gen:
    print(item)
# Output: 1, 2, 3
```

You can also manually call the generator's next() method to get the next value.

```python
gen = my_generator()
print(next(gen))  # Output: 1
print(next(gen))  # Output: 2
print(next(gen))  # Output: 3
# Calling next() again will raise StopIteration since the
generator is exhausted.
```

Infinite Generators:

One of the most powerful aspects of generators is their ability to create infinite sequences. Since they produce values lazily, you can create a generator that never ends, which can be useful in certain scenarios.

```python
def infinite_generator():
    i = 1
    while True:
        yield i
        i += 1


gen = infinite_generator()
print(next(gen))  # Output: 1
print(next(gen))  # Output: 2
# This will keep printing the next values indefinitely until
you stop the loop manually.
```

Generator Expressions:

In addition to defining generator functions, you can also use generator expressions, which have a similar syntax to list comprehensions but with parentheses instead of square brackets. Generator expressions are more memory-efficient since they produce values on-the-fly, without creating a full list.

```python
# Generator expression
gen = (x ** 2 for x in range(10))
for item in gen:
    print(item)
```

```
# Output: 0, 1, 4, 9, 16, 25, 36, 49, 64, 81
```

Generators are incredibly useful when dealing with large datasets or when generating values on-the-fly, saving memory and improving performance. They are especially handy in scenarios where you don't need to access the entire sequence of values simultaneously. By understanding and effectively using generators, you can optimize your Python code and make it more efficient.

11. Decorators:

11.1. FUNCTION DECORATORS

11.2. CLASS DECORATORS

11.1. FUNCTION DECORATORS

Function decorators in Python are a powerful and flexible feature that allows you to modify the behavior of functions by wrapping them with another function. Decorators provide a way to extend the functionality of functions without changing their code, promoting code reusability and making it easier to add common functionalities across multiple functions.

In Python, a decorator is implemented using the "@" symbol followed by the name of the decorator function. When a function is decorated, it is passed as an argument to the decorator function, and the decorator function returns a new function (or a callable) that replaces the original function.

```
@decorator_function
def original_function():
    # Function implementation
```

Define the Decorator Function:

A decorator function is an ordinary function that takes another function as its argument. It performs some actions before or after calling the original function and returns a new function that replaces the original one. The decorator can add additional functionalities, modify the behavior of the original function, or perform tasks such as logging, caching, or input validation.

```python
def my_decorator(original_function):
    def wrapper():
        # Code to be executed before the original function is
called
        print("Something is happening before the function is
called.")
        # Call the original function
        result = original_function()
        # Code to be executed after the original function is
called
        print("Something is happening after the function is
called.")
        # Return the result of the original function
        return result

    # Return the wrapper function
    return wrapper
```

Decorate the Original Function:

To apply the decorator to a function, use the "@" symbol
followed by the name of the decorator function directly
above the original function definition.

```python
@my_decorator
def say_hello():
    print("Hello!")
```

Call the Decorated Function:

When you call the decorated function, it is actually the wrapper() function returned by the decorator that gets executed. The wrapper() function, in turn, calls the original function within its own execution flow.

```
say_hello()


#Output:
Something is happening before the function is called.
Hello!
Something is happening after the function is called.
```

In this example, the say_hello() function is decorated with the my_decorator function. When say_hello() is called, it actually invokes the wrapper() function, which adds some additional behavior before and after calling the original say_hello() function.

Decorators are widely used for various purposes, such as:

- Logging: To log function calls, their arguments, and results.
- Caching: To cache function results to speed up future calls with the same arguments.
- Authorization: To add authentication and authorization checks before executing a function.

- Input Validation: To validate the input arguments of a function before execution.

You can use multiple decorators on a single function, and decorators can take arguments themselves, making them highly flexible and versatile in Python. Understanding and using decorators is a key skill for writing clean, maintainable, and extensible Python code.

11.2. CLASS DECORATORS

Object-Oriented Programming (OOP) is a powerful paradigm in software development that organizes code into classes and objects, promoting code reusability and maintainability. Python, being an object-oriented language, provides various features to support OOP principles. Class decorators are a fundamental aspect of Python that enables programmers to extend the behaviour of classes, making them more flexible and dynamic. In this section, we will delve into the world of class decorators, exploring their purpose, syntax, and practical applications.

Introduction to Decorators

Before we delve into class decorators, let's briefly introduce decorators in Python. Decorators are a powerful feature of Python that allows functions (and methods) to be modified or extended by other functions. They follow a simple concept: a decorator function wraps around another function, providing additional functionality without modifying its source code directly.

```python
def add(a, b):
    return a + b

result = add(2, 3)
print(result)  # Output: 5
```

Now, let's create a decorator function that prints a message before and after calling the original function:

```python
def decorator(func):
    def wrapper(*args, **kwargs):
        print("Before function execution.")
        result = func(*args, **kwargs)
        print("After function execution.")
        return result
    return wrapper


@decorator
def add(a, b):
    return a + b


result = add(2, 3)
print(result)  # Output:
# Before function execution.
# After function execution.
# 5
```

The @decorator syntax is a shorthand for applying the decorator to the add function. In this example, the decorator function wraps around the add function, adding the before-and-after print statements.

Introducing Class Decorators

Class decorators follow a similar concept to function decorators but apply their magic to classes instead of functions. A class decorator is a function that takes a class as an argument, extends or modifies the class, and returns the updated class.

In Python, the syntax to apply a class decorator is similar to function decorators, using the @decorator notation directly above the class definition.

```python
def decorator(cls):
    class NewClass(cls):
        def new_method(self):
            print("This is a new method.")

    return NewClass

@decorator
class OriginalClass:
    def existing_method(self):
        print("This is an existing method.")

obj = OriginalClass()
obj.existing_method()  # Output: This is an existing method.
obj.new_method()       # Output: This is a new method.
```

In this example, the decorator function takes the OriginalClass as an argument, creates a new class called NewClass, adds a new method new_method, and returns the updated class. The @decorator syntax then replaces OriginalClass with NewClass, effectively enhancing the class's functionality.

Use Cases and Benefits of Class Decorators

Class decorators offer several advantages and use cases, making them a valuable tool in Python development. Here are some key benefits:

1. Code Reusability

Class decorators enable developers to encapsulate commonly used functionalities and apply them to multiple classes. This promotes code reusability and reduces the need to duplicate code across different classes.

2. Mixin Functionality

A common use case for class decorators is implementing mixin functionality. Mixins are a way to add a specific set of features to multiple classes without using inheritance. They allow for better code organization and avoid deep class hierarchies, which can be challenging to maintain.

```python
class JSONMixin:
    def to_json(self):
        import json
        return json.dumps(self.__dict__)


@JSONMixin
class Person:
    def __init__(self, name, age):
```

```python
        self.name = name
        self.age = age

person = Person("Alice", 30)
print(person.to_json())
# Output: {"name": "Alice", "age": 30}
```

In this example, the JSONMixin class decorator adds the to_json method to the Person class, enabling it to convert its attributes to a JSON string.

3. Adding Properties and Attributes

Class decorators can be used to add properties and attributes to classes dynamically. This can be useful when you want to extend a class's functionality without modifying its source code or when working with third-party libraries and classes.

4. Validation and Error Handling

You can create class decorators that validate the input to class methods or handle exceptions globally. This centralizes error handling logic, making the code more maintainable and readable.

5. Performance Profiling

Class decorators can be used to measure the execution time

of class methods, providing insights into performance bottlenecks and optimizations.

6. Caching

You can implement caching mechanisms using class decorators to store results of expensive computations, saving time and resources when the same computations are requested again.

Implementing Class Decorators

Creating class decorators in Python involves defining a decorator function that takes a class as an argument, returns an updated class, and then applying the decorator using the @decorator syntax. Here's a step-by-step guide to implement a class decorator:

Step 1: Define the Decorator Function

First, define the decorator function that takes the class as its argument. The decorator can extend the class, add new methods, modify existing methods, or perform any desired changes.

```
def decorator(cls):
    # Perform modifications to the class here.
    # You can create a new class that inherits from the
original class
    # and add new methods, properties, or attributes to it.
```

```
    # Return the updated class.
    return cls
```

Step 2: Apply the Decorator

Next, apply the decorator to a class using the @decorator syntax directly above the class definition. This indicates that the decorator function should be called with the class as its argument, and the result should replace the original class.

```
@decorator
class OriginalClass:
    # Class methods, properties, and attributes go here.
```

Step 3: Test the Decorated Class

Finally, create instances of the decorated class and test its methods and attributes to ensure that the decorator worked as expected.

```
obj = OriginalClass()
# Test class methods and properties here.
```

Class decorators in Python offer a powerful way to enhance object-oriented programming. By extending classes dynamically, class decorators provide code reusability, mixin functionality, validation, error handling, and much more. With a good understanding of class decorators, you can write more flexible and maintainable code, making your Python projects more efficient and robust.

12. Working with Dates and Times:

- ## Date and time manipulation (datetime module)

Date and time manipulation (datetime module)

Date and time manipulation is a crucial aspect of programming, especially when dealing with tasks that involve scheduling, event tracking, or data analysis over specific time intervals. In Python, the datetime module provides a rich set of functionalities to work with dates, times, and timedeltas. It simplifies date and time operations, making it easier for developers to handle various temporal aspects of their applications. In this section, we will explore the datetime module and its essential features for date and time manipulation in Python.

Importing the datetime Module

Before we delve into the functionalities of the datetime module, let's start by importing it into our Python script:

```
import datetime
```

Creating Date and Time Objects

The datetime module offers several classes to represent dates and times. The primary classes are:

- ***datetime.date:*** Represents a date (year, month, day).

- ***datetime.time:*** Represents a time of day (hour, minute, second, microsecond).
- ***datetime.datetime***: Represents both date and time (year, month, day, hour, minute, second, microsecond).
- ***datetime.timedelta:*** Represents the difference between two dates or times.

Creating Date Objects

To create a date object, you can use the datetime.date class constructor, passing the year, month, and day as arguments:

```python
# Creating a date object for July 4, 2023
date_obj = datetime.date(2023, 7, 4)
print(date_obj)  # Output: 2023-07-04
```

Creating Time Objects

For time objects, you can use the datetime.time class constructor, passing the hour, minute, second, and microsecond as arguments:

```python
# Creating a time object for 12:34:56.789
time_obj = datetime.time(12, 34, 56, 789000)
print(time_obj)  # Output: 12:34:56.789000
```

Creating DateTime Objects

To create a datetime object that combines date and time, you can use the datetime.datetime class constructor:

```python
# Creating a datetime object for December 25, 2023, at
09:15:30
datetime_obj = datetime.datetime(2023, 12, 25, 9, 15, 30)
print(datetime_obj)  # Output: 2023-12-25 09:15:30
```

Current Date and Time

The datetime module also provides functions to retrieve the
current date and time from the system clock:

```python
# Current date
current_date = datetime.date.today()
print(current_date)  # Output: Today's date in the format:
YYYY-MM-DD

# Current time
current_time = datetime.datetime.now().time()
print(current_time)  # Output: Current time in the format:
HH:MM:SS.microseconds
```

Formatting and Parsing Dates and Times

The strftime method of datetime objects allows you to format
dates and times into strings, while the strptime function
enables you to parse strings into datetime objects.

Formatting Dates and Times

```python
# Formatting a datetime object as a custom string
datetime_obj = datetime.datetime(2023, 9, 15, 18, 30, 45)
```

```python
formatted_str = datetime_obj.strftime("%Y-%m-%d
%H:%M:%S")
print(formatted_str)  # Output: "2023-09-15 18:30:45"
```

Parsing Dates and Times

```python
# Parsing a string into a datetime object
date_str = "2023-09-15 18:30:45"
parsed_datetime = datetime.datetime.strptime(date_str,
"%Y-%m-%d %H:%M:%S")
print(parsed_datetime)  # Output: 2023-09-15 18:30:45
```

Date and Time Arithmetic

The datetime module provides functionalities for performing arithmetic operations on dates and times using timedelta objects.

Calculating Time Differences (Timedeltas)

You can calculate the difference between two dates or times using timedelta. This is useful for finding the duration between events or adding/subtracting intervals to dates.

```python
# Calculating the time difference between two dates
date1 = datetime.date(2023, 8, 20)
date2 = datetime.date(2023, 9, 15)
time_difference = date2 - date1
print(time_difference.days)
# Output: 26 (number of days between the two dates)
```

```python
# Adding a timedelta to a datetime object
datetime_obj = datetime.datetime(2023, 9, 15, 12, 0, 0)
time_delta = datetime.timedelta(hours=3, minutes=30)
new_datetime_obj = datetime_obj + time_delta
print(new_datetime_obj)  # Output: 2023-09-15 15:30:00
```

Timezone Support

The datetime module also includes limited support for
working with time zones through the pytz library. This allows
you to handle datetime objects with respect to different time
zones, accounting for daylight saving time and other
timezone-specific rules.

To use pytz, you need to install it separately:

```
pip install pytz
```

After installing pytz, you can use it to create timezone-aware datetime objects:

```python
import pytz

# Create a timezone-aware datetime object
utc_datetime = datetime.datetime(2023, 9, 15, 12, 0, 0,
tzinfo=pytz.UTC)
print(utc_datetime)
# Output: 2023-09-15 12:00:00+00:00

# Convert timezone-aware datetime to a different timezone
local_timezone = pytz.timezone("America/New_York")
```

```python
local_datetime = utc_datetime.astimezone(local_timezone)
print(local_datetime)
# Output: 2023-09-15 08:00:00-04:00 (assuming daylight
saving time)
```

The datetime module in Python provides a comprehensive set of tools for date and time manipulation. By using its classes and functions, developers can handle various temporal operations, format dates and times, calculate time differences, and even work with time zones. Whether you're building web applications, data analysis tools, or scheduling systems, the datetime module is an essential part of any Python programmer's toolkit. Its flexibility and ease of use make it a valuable resource for dealing with date and time-related tasks efficiently.

13. Python Standard Library:

- **Exploring commonly used modules (os, sys, math, random, etc.)**

Exploring commonly used modules (os, sys, math, random, etc.)

In Python, modules are pre-written code libraries that provide a wide range of functionalities to enhance the language's capabilities. These modules extend Python's core features and allow developers to perform various tasks efficiently. In this section, we will explore some commonly used modules in Python, including os, sys, math, random, and more, highlighting their key functionalities and use cases.

1. os Module

The os module provides functions for interacting with the operating system, allowing you to work with files, directories, and environment variables.

Key Functionalities:

- File and Directory Operations: The os module provides functions like os.listdir(), os.path.exists(), os.path.join(), os.mkdir(), and os.remove() for working with files and directories.
- Environment Variables: You can access and modify environment variables using os.environ.

- Process Management: The os module also includes functionalities to interact with processes, such as os.system() and os.spawn*().

```python
import os

# List all files and directories in the current directory
files = os.listdir(".")
print(files)

# Check if a file exists
if os.path.exists("example.txt"):
    print("File exists.")
else:
    print("File does not exist.")

# Get the value of an environment variable
print(os.environ.get("PATH"))
```

2. sys Module

The sys module provides functions and variables to interact with the Python interpreter and system-specific functionalities.

Key Functionalities:

- Command Line Arguments: You can access command-line arguments passed to the script using sys.argv.

- System Information: The sys module offers variables like sys.platform and sys.version to get information about the system and Python version, respectively.
- Standard Streams: sys.stdin, sys.stdout, and sys.stderr represent the standard input, output, and error streams, allowing you to redirect them if needed.

```python
import sys

# Access command-line arguments
print("Script name:", sys.argv[0])
print("Arguments:", sys.argv[1:])

# Get Python version
print("Python version:", sys.version)

# Redirect stdout to a file
with open("output.txt", "w") as f:
    sys.stdout = f
    print("This will be written to output.txt")
    sys.stdout = sys.__stdout__  # Reset stdout to default
```

3. *math Module*

The math module provides mathematical functions and constants for performing various numeric operations.

Key Functionalities:

- Basic Arithmetic: The math module offers functions like math.sqrt(), math.pow(), math.floor(), math.ceil(), and math.round() for common arithmetic operations.
- Trigonometric Functions: You can use math.sin(), math.cos(), math.tan(), math.degrees(), and math.radians() for trigonometric calculations.
- Constants: math.pi and math.e represent the mathematical constants π (pi) and e, respectively.

```python
import math

# Calculate the square root and power
print("Square root:", math.sqrt(25))
print("2 to the power of 3:", math.pow(2, 3))

# Trigonometric functions
print("Sine of 30 degrees:", math.sin(math.radians(30)))
print("Cosine of 45 degrees:", math.cos(math.radians(45)))

# Mathematical constants
print("Value of π (pi):", math.pi)
print("Value of e:", math.e)
```

4. *random* Module

The random module allows you to work with random numbers and make selections randomly.

Key Functionalities:

- Generating Random Numbers: Functions like random.random(), random.randint(), random.uniform(), and random.randrange() generate random numbers within specified ranges.
- Making Random Choices: You can randomly select elements from lists or sequences using random.choice() and shuffle elements using random.shuffle().

```python
import random

# Generate random float between 0 and 1
print("Random float:", random.random())

# Generate random integer between 1 and 10
print("Random integer:", random.randint(1, 10))

# Make random choice from a list
fruits = ["apple", "banana", "orange", "grape", "kiwi"]
print("Random fruit:", random.choice(fruits))

# Shuffle elements in a list
random.shuffle(fruits)
print("Shuffled fruits:", fruits)
```

The os, sys, math, random, and other commonly used modules in Python offer an extensive range of functionalities to simplify various tasks. By leveraging these modules, developers can work efficiently with files, directories, system information, mathematical calculations, and random numbers. Understanding these modules and their key features is essential for proficient Python programming and can significantly enhance your productivity as a developer.

Let's add some additional points about each of the commonly used modules:

1. os Module:

- Directory Navigation: The os module allows you to change the current working directory using os.chdir() and get the current working directory with os.getcwd().

- File Permissions: You can set file permissions using os.chmod() and check file permissions with os.access().

- Platform-Specific Functionality: The os module provides functions like os.name and os.sep to retrieve platform-specific information, such as the name of the operating system and the path separator.

2. *sys Module:*

- System Exit: The sys.exit() function allows you to terminate the Python interpreter with an optional exit status.

- Module Importing: You can manipulate the module search path using sys.path, allowing you to add custom directories for module imports.

- Recursion Limit: The sys.setrecursionlimit() function lets you set the maximum recursion depth in Python to avoid stack overflows.

3. *math Module:*

- Trigonometric Inverse Functions: The math.acos(), math.asin(), and math.atan() functions provide the inverse trigonometric calculations.

- Logarithmic Functions: The math.log(), math.log10(), and math.log2() functions allow you to perform logarithmic calculations.

- Rounding Functions: The math.floor() and math.ceil() functions provide floor and ceiling rounding, respectively, while math.trunc() truncates towards zero.

4. *random Module:*

- Random Seed: You can set a random seed using random.seed() to ensure reproducibility in random number generation.

- Random Sampling: The random.sample() function allows you to sample elements from a sequence without replacement, while random.choices() samples with replacement.

- Probability Distribution: The random.gauss() function generates random numbers following a Gaussian (normal) distribution.

5. *datetime Module:*

- Date Formatting and Parsing: Besides strftime and strptime, the datetime module also offers the date.fromisoformat() and datetime.fromisoformat() methods for parsing ISO-formatted strings into date and datetime objects, respectively.

- Timezone Awareness: In addition to pytz, Python 3.9 introduced the zoneinfo module, providing timezone support without the need for a third-party library.

- Date Arithmetic: The date and datetime objects support arithmetic operations such as addition, subtraction, and comparisons, allowing you to work with time intervals easily.

6. collections Module:

- Namedtuple: The collections.namedtuple() function creates simple classes with named fields, acting as memory-efficient alternatives to regular classes.

- Counter: The collections.Counter() class provides a fast and efficient way to count occurrences of elements in a collection.

- Defaultdict: The collections.defaultdict() class is a subclass of the built-in dict that returns a default value when accessing a nonexistent key.

7. json Module:

- Serialization and Deserialization: The json module allows you to convert Python objects to JSON strings (json.dumps()) and JSON strings to Python objects (json.loads()).

- Custom Serialization: You can implement custom serialization and deserialization using the json.JSONEncoder and json.JSONDecoder classes.

- File Handling: The json module provides functions like json.dump() and json.load() to work directly with JSON files.

8. time Module:

- Time Measurements: The time module provides functions like time.time() and time.perf_counter() to measure time intervals and performance.

- Sleep: You can introduce delays in your code using time.sleep().

- Time Formatting: The time.strftime() function allows you to format time as a string.

Understanding and utilizing these commonly used modules in Python can significantly improve your productivity as a developer. Each module provides a set of powerful functionalities that simplify various tasks, from file operations and system interactions (os, sys) to mathematical computations (math) and random number generation (random). Additionally, modules like datetime, collections, json, and time offer specialized features to handle dates, data structures, JSON serialization, and time-related tasks effectively. By leveraging these modules, you can build robust, efficient, and feature-rich Python applications.

14. Working with Databases:

14.1. SQL (SQLite)

14.2. Database connectivity (SQLite3)

14.1. SQL (SQLite)

SQL (Structured Query Language) is a domain-specific language used for managing and manipulating relational databases. It provides a standardized way to interact with databases, allowing users to create, update, and query data in a structured manner. SQLite is a lightweight, serverless, self-contained, and embedded relational database management system (RDBMS) that implements SQL. In this section, we will explore SQL and its implementation in SQLite, discussing its key features, data manipulation, and database operations.

Introduction to SQL

SQL is widely used for database management and is the backbone of relational database systems. It allows users to perform various operations on databases, such as creating tables, inserting data, querying data, updating records, and deleting data. SQL uses a declarative syntax, meaning you specify what you want to achieve, and the database engine figures out how to execute the operation efficiently.

SQL statements generally fall into the following categories:

- Data Definition Language (DDL): Used for defining database structure and schema. Common DDL statements include CREATE, ALTER, DROP, and RENAME.

- Data Manipulation Language (DML): Used for manipulating data in the database. Common DML statements include INSERT, SELECT, UPDATE, and DELETE.

- Data Control Language (DCL): Used for managing access to data. Common DCL statements include GRANT, REVOKE, and DENY.

- Transaction Control Language (TCL): Used for managing transactions in the database. Common TCL statements include COMMIT, ROLLBACK, and SAVEPOINT.

Introduction to SQLite

SQLite is a popular, lightweight, and self-contained RDBMS that is widely used in various applications, including mobile apps, desktop software, and web applications. It is serverless, meaning it doesn't require a separate database server to operate. Instead, it stores the entire database as a single file on the disk, making it easy to set up and manage. SQLite is written in C and is designed to be fast, reliable, and efficient.

Key Features of SQLite:

- Zero Configuration: SQLite doesn't require any configuration or setup; it is ready to use "out of the box."

- Cross-Platform: SQLite is cross-platform and can run on various operating systems, including Windows, macOS, Linux, and mobile platforms like Android and iOS.

- ACID Properties: SQLite supports ACID (Atomicity, Consistency, Isolation, Durability) properties, ensuring data integrity and reliability.

- Single Database File: The entire database is contained in a single file, making it easy to transfer and manage.

- Low Memory Footprint: SQLite is designed to be memory-efficient, making it suitable for embedded systems and resource-constrained environments.

- Full SQL Support: SQLite implements a large subset of SQL92 standard, providing a rich set of SQL functionalities.

Using SQLite with Python

To work with SQLite in Python, you need to use the sqlite3 module, which comes pre-installed with Python.

Connecting to a Database

```python
import sqlite3

# Connect to an SQLite database or create one if it doesn't exist
conn = sqlite3.connect("example.db")
```

Creating a Table and Inserting Data

```python
# Create a table
conn.execute('''CREATE TABLE IF NOT EXISTS users (
        id INTEGER PRIMARY KEY,
        name TEXT NOT NULL,
        age INTEGER)''')

# Insert data into the table
conn.execute("INSERT INTO users (name, age) VALUES (?, ?)", ("Nibe", 20))
conn.execute("INSERT INTO users (name, age) VALUES (?, ?)", ("Dita", 21))
```

```python
# Commit changes
conn.commit()
```

Querying Data

```python
# Query data from the table
cursor = conn.execute("SELECT * FROM users WHERE age > ?", (25,))
rows = cursor.fetchall()

for row in rows:
    print(f"ID: {row[0]}, Name: {row[1]}, Age: {row[2]}")
```

Updating and Deleting Data

```python
# Update data
conn.execute("UPDATE users SET age = ? WHERE name = ?", (26, "Dita"))
conn.commit()

# Delete data
conn.execute("DELETE FROM users WHERE name = ?", ("Nibe",))
conn.commit()
```

Closing the Connection

```python
# Close the connection
conn.close()
```

SQL (Structured Query Language) is a powerful language for managing relational databases, allowing users to perform various operations on data in a structured and efficient manner. SQLite, as a lightweight and serverless RDBMS, provides an excellent choice for small to medium-scale applications, offering cross-platform support and easy integration with Python. By using the sqlite3 module in Python, developers can effortlessly work with SQLite databases and build robust, data-driven applications.

14.2. Database connectivity (SQLite3)

Database connectivity refers to the process of establishing a connection between a programming language (such as Python) and a database management system (DBMS) like SQLite. This allows the programming language to interact with the database, perform various operations (e.g., querying, inserting, updating, and deleting data), and retrieve results from the database.

In this section, we will explore database connectivity using SQLite3 in Python. SQLite3 is a lightweight, serverless, and self-contained relational database management system that comes with Python's standard library, making it easy to work with databases without the need for any external installations.

Establishing Database Connection

To connect to an SQLite database using Python, you need to use the sqlite3 module, which comes pre-installed with Python. The main class in this module is sqlite3.Connection, which represents the connection to the database.

```
import sqlite3
```

```python
# Connect to an SQLite database or create one if it doesn't
exist
conn = sqlite3.connect("example.db")
```

In this example, we connect to an SQLite database named
"example.db." If the database doesn't exist, SQLite will create
it automatically.

Creating a Table and Inserting Data

Once the connection is established, you can interact with the
database by creating tables and inserting data.

```python
# Create a table
conn.execute('''CREATE TABLE IF NOT EXISTS users (
        id INTEGER PRIMARY KEY,
        name TEXT NOT NULL,
        age INTEGER)''')

# Insert data into the table
conn.execute("INSERT INTO users (name, age) VALUES (?,
?)", ("Alice", 30))
conn.execute("INSERT INTO users (name, age) VALUES (?,
?)", ("Bob", 25))

# Commit changes
conn.commit()
```

In this example, we create a table named "users" with
columns "id," "name," and "age." We then insert two rows of

data into the table using parameterized queries to prevent SQL injection.

Querying Data

To retrieve data from the database, you can use SQL queries. The execute() method is used to execute SQL commands, and the fetchall() method is used to retrieve the results.

```python
# Query data from the table
cursor = conn.execute("SELECT * FROM users WHERE age > ?", (25,))
rows = cursor.fetchall()

for row in rows:
    print(f"ID: {row[0]}, Name: {row[1]}, Age: {row[2]}")
```

In this example, we execute a SELECT query to retrieve users with an age greater than 25 and then print the results.

Updating and Deleting Data

To update or delete data in the database, you can use the execute() method with appropriate UPDATE or DELETE queries.

```python
# Update data
conn.execute("UPDATE users SET age = ? WHERE name = ?", (26, "Alice"))
conn.commit()
```

```python
# Delete data
conn.execute("DELETE FROM users WHERE name = ?",
("Bob",))
conn.commit()
```

In this example, we update Alice's age to 26 and then delete Bob's record from the "users" table.

Closing the Connection

After you have completed the database operations, it's essential to close the connection to the database.

```python
# Close the connection
conn.close()
```

Closing the connection ensures that any changes made to the database are committed, and resources are released.

Database connectivity with SQLite3 in Python allows you to interact with SQLite databases, create tables, insert, update, and delete data, and retrieve query results. SQLite's lightweight nature and integration with Python make it an excellent choice for small to medium-scale applications where a full-fledged database server is not required. With the sqlite3 module, you can easily perform various database operations in your Python projects and build robust, data-driven applications.

15. Regular Expressions:

- **PATTERN MATCHING AND TEXT MANIPULATION (RE MODULE)**

Pattern matching and text manipulation (re module)

Pattern matching and text manipulation are essential tasks in programming, allowing developers to search for specific patterns within text and perform various operations based on those patterns. The re module in Python provides powerful functionalities for regular expression-based pattern matching and text manipulation. Regular expressions (regex) are sequences of characters that define a search pattern, allowing you to perform complex text operations efficiently.

In this section, we will explore the re module in Python and its key functions for pattern matching and text manipulation.

Importing the re Module

Before using the re module, you need to import it into your Python script:

```
import re
```

Basic Pattern Matching

The re module offers several functions to work with regular expressions. Let's start with some basic pattern matching examples:

1. re.match()

The re.match() function searches for the pattern at the beginning of the string and returns a match object if the pattern is found.

```
pattern = r"Hello"
text = "Hello, World!"
match = re.match(pattern, text)

if match:
    print("Pattern found:", match.group())
else:
    print("Pattern not found.")
```

2. re.search()

The re.search() function searches for the pattern throughout the entire string and returns the first match it finds.

```
pattern = r"World"
text = "Hello, World!"
match = re.search(pattern, text)

if match:
    print("Pattern found:", match.group())
else:
    print("Pattern not found.")
```

3. re.findall()

The re.findall() function returns all occurrences of the pattern as a list of strings.

```python
pattern = r"\d+"
text = "The price is $100 and $50"
matches = re.findall(pattern, text)


print("Matches:", matches)
```

Regular Expression Patterns

Regular expressions allow you to define complex patterns using special characters and metacharacters. Some commonly used metacharacters are:

- . : Matches any character except a newline.
- * : Matches zero or more occurrences of the previous character.
- + : Matches one or more occurrences of the previous character.
- ? : Matches zero or one occurrence of the previous character.
- ^ : Matches the beginning of a string.
- $: Matches the end of a string.
- [ ] : Matches any character inside the square brackets.
- [^] : Matches any character not inside the square brackets.
- ( ) : Groups expressions together.

Text Manipulation with re

The re module also provides functions for text manipulation using regular expressions.

1. re.sub()

The re.sub() function allows you to replace occurrences of a pattern with a specified string.

```python
pattern = r"\d+"
text = "The price is $100 and $50"
new_text = re.sub(pattern, "X", text)

print("Modified text:", new_text)
```

2. re.split()

The re.split() function splits a string by the occurrences of a pattern and returns a list of substrings.

```python
pattern = r"\s+"
text = "Hello  World   Python"
words = re.split(pattern, text)

print("Words:", words)
```

Flags in re

The re module also supports flags that modify the behavior of regular expression functions.

1. re.IGNORECASE or re.I

This flag enables case-insensitive matching.

```python
pattern = r"hello"
text = "Hello, World!"
match = re.search(pattern, text, re.IGNORECASE)

if match:
    print("Pattern found:", match.group())
else:
    print("Pattern not found.")
```


2. re.MULTILINE or re.M

This flag enables multi-line matching.

```python
pattern = r"^Hello"
text = "Hello, World!\nHello, Python!"
matches = re.findall(pattern, text, re.MULTILINE)

print("Matches:", matches)
```


The re module in Python is a powerful tool for pattern matching and text manipulation using regular expressions. It allows you to search for specific patterns, extract data from text, and perform various text operations efficiently. By mastering regular expressions and understanding the functions provided by the re module, you can handle complex text processing tasks in Python effectively.

16. Debugging and Testing:

16.1. Debugging techniques and tools (pdb)

16.2. Unit testing (unittest module)

16.1. DEBUGGING TECHNIQUES AND TOOLS (PDB)

Debugging is a crucial aspect of software development that involves identifying and fixing errors or issues in a program. Python provides several debugging techniques and tools to help developers diagnose and resolve problems effectively. One of the most commonly used debugging tools in Python is the Python Debugger (pdb), which is a built-in interactive debugger. In this section, we will explore debugging techniques and how to use pdb to debug Python programs.

Debugging Techniques

1. Print Statements

Print statements are one of the simplest and oldest debugging techniques. You can insert print statements in your code to display the values of variables and the flow of execution at specific points.

```python
def calculate_sum(a, b):
    print("Entering calculate_sum function")
    print(f"a: {a}, b: {b}")
    result = a + b
```

```python
    print("Exiting calculate_sum function")
    return result
```

2. Logging

Logging is a more sophisticated debugging technique where you use the logging module to log messages at different log levels (e.g., DEBUG, INFO, WARNING, ERROR) to analyze the program's behavior.

```python
import logging

logging.basicConfig(level=logging.DEBUG)

def calculate_sum(a, b):
    logging.debug("Entering calculate_sum function")
    logging.debug(f"a: {a}, b: {b}")
    result = a + b
    logging.debug("Exiting calculate_sum function")
    return result
```

3. Assertion

Assertions are used to check if a condition holds true at a specific point in the program. If the condition is False, an AssertionError is raised, indicating a problem in the code.

```python
def divide(a, b):
    assert b != 0, "Division by zero is not allowed."
    return a / b
```

Using pdb for Debugging

Python's built-in debugger pdb provides an interactive debugging environment that allows you to step through your code, inspect variables, and analyze the program's flow. Here's how to use pdb:

1. Importing pdb

```
import pdb
```

2. Setting Breakpoints

You can set breakpoints in your code using the pdb.set_trace() function. When the interpreter reaches this point, it will pause the execution, and the pdb interactive prompt will be activated.

```python
def calculate_sum(a, b):
    result = a + b
    pdb.set_trace()
    return result
```

3. Running the Debugger

You can run your script with the -m pdb option, or use the pdb.run() function to start the debugger.

- _Bash:_

```bash
python -m pdb your_script.py
```

- ***Python:***

```python
import pdb

def main():
    # Your code here

if __name__ == "__main__":
    pdb.run("main()")
```

4. Pdb Commands

Once the debugger is active, you can use various pdb commands to interact with the program:

- n or next: Execute the current line of code.
- s or step: Step into a function call.
- c or continue: Continue execution until the next breakpoint or end of the program.
- l or list: Display the source code around the current line.
- p or print: Print the value of a variable.
- b or break: Set a breakpoint at a specific line number.
- q or quit: Quit the debugger and exit the program.

5. Exiting the Debugger

To exit the debugger, use the q or quit command. If you want to continue execution without debugging, use the c or continue command until the end of the program or the next breakpoint.

Debugging is an essential skill for every programmer. By employing techniques like print statements, logging, and assertions, you can gain insights into your program's behavior and identify potential issues. The pdb interactive debugger in Python provides a powerful tool for stepping through code, inspecting variables, and analyzing program flow. By mastering debugging techniques and using tools like pdb, you can effectively diagnose and resolve problems in your Python programs, leading to more robust and reliable software. Happy debugging!

16.2. UNIT TESTING (UNITTEST MODULE)

Unit testing is a software testing technique that involves testing individual units or components of a program in isolation to ensure they work as expected. The unittest module in Python is a built-in testing framework that provides tools for writing and running unit tests. It allows developers to define test cases, run tests, and automatically discover and execute test methods.

In this section, we will explore the unittest module in Python and learn how to write and run unit tests for Python code.

Creating Test Cases

A test case in the unittest module is a subclass of unittest.TestCase that contains one or more test methods. Each test method should test a specific aspect of the code under test. Test method names must start with the word "test" to be recognized as test cases.

- **Python:**

```python
import unittest
```

```python
def add(a, b):
    return a + b

class TestAddFunction(unittest.TestCase):

    def test_add_positive_numbers(self):
        result = add(3, 5)
        self.assertEqual(result, 8)

    def test_add_negative_numbers(self):
        result = add(-2, -3)
        self.assertEqual(result, -5)

    def test_add_zero(self):
        result = add(10, 0)
        self.assertEqual(result, 10)

if __name__ == '__main__':
    unittest.main()
```

In this example, we define a test case TestAddFunction that contains three test methods, each testing a different scenario for the add function.

Running Unit Tests

To run the unit tests defined in a module, you can use the unittest test runner. If your test case is defined in a file named test_module.py, you can run the tests from the command line using:

• *Bash:*

```
python -m unittest test_module.py
```

The test runner will automatically discover test cases and test methods and execute them.

Assertions

The unittest module provides several assertion methods to verify the expected behavior of the code being tested. Some commonly used assertions are:

- assertEqual(a, b): Checks if a and b are equal.
- assertNotEqual(a, b): Checks if a and b are not equal.
- assertTrue(expr): Checks if expr is true.
- assertFalse(expr): Checks if expr is false.
- assertIs(a, b): Checks if a is the same object as b.
- assertIsNot(a, b): Checks if a is not the same object as b.
- assertIsNone(expr): Checks if expr is None.
- assertIsNotNone(expr): Checks if expr is not None.
- assertIn(a, b): Checks if a is in b.
- assertNotIn(a, b): Checks if a is not in b.
- assertRaises(exception, callable, *args, **kwargs): Checks if calling callable with args and kwargs raises an exception of type exception

Test Discovery

The unittest module can automatically discover and run all test cases defined in multiple files within a directory. To do this, you can run the test discovery from the command line:

- **Bash:**

```
python -m unittest discover directory
```

The test runner will search for all files named test*.py in the specified directory and run all the tests found.

Test Fixtures

Test fixtures are setup and teardown actions that are performed before and after running each test method. The unittest module provides setUp() and tearDown() methods in a test case to define fixtures.

- **Python:**

```python
import unittest

class TestMathOperations(unittest.TestCase):

    def setUp(self):
        # Perform setup actions here (e.g., initializing resources)
        pass
```

```python
    def tearDown(self):
        # Perform teardown actions here (e.g., releasing resources)
        pass

    def test_addition(self):
        # Test addition operation here
        pass

    def test_subtraction(self):
        # Test subtraction operation here
        pass

if __name__ == '__main__':
    unittest.main()
```

The setUp() method is called before each test method, and the tearDown() method is called after each test method.

The unittest module in Python provides a powerful testing framework for writing and running unit tests. By creating test cases with test methods and using assertions to verify the expected behavior, developers can ensure that their code works as intended and identify potential issues. Additionally, test discovery and fixtures in unittest make it easy to organize and manage tests for larger projects. Embracing unit testing practices can lead to more robust, reliable, and maintainable Python code. Happy testing!

17. Performance Optimization:

- **PROFILING AND OPTIMIZING CODE (TIMEIT, CPROFILE)**

Profiling and optimizing code (timeit, cProfile)

Profiling and optimizing code are crucial steps in software development to ensure that programs run efficiently and meet performance requirements. Python provides built-in modules like timeit and cProfile that help developers profile code execution time and identify performance bottlenecks. In this article, we will explore these modules and learn how to use them to profile and optimize Python code effectively.

Profiling with timeit

The timeit module is used to measure the execution time of small code snippets. It is particularly useful for comparing the performance of different implementations or approaches.

Timing a Function

To time a specific function or code snippet, you can use the timeit.timeit() function.

- **Python:**

```python
import timeit

def factorial_recursive(n):
    if n <= 1:
```

```python
        return 1
    return n * factorial_recursive(n - 1)

time_taken = timeit.timeit("factorial_recursive(10)",
globals=globals(), number=10000)
average_time = time_taken / 10000
print("Average time taken:", average_time, "seconds")
```

In this example, we measure the average execution time of the factorial_recursive function to calculate the factorial of 10 over 10,000 iterations.

Timing Multiple Functions

You can also time multiple functions or code snippets using the timeit.Timer class.

- ***Python:***

```python
import timeit

def factorial_iterative(n):
    result = 1
    for i in range(1, n + 1):
        result *= i
    return result

t = timeit.Timer("factorial_recursive(10)", globals=globals())
time_recursive = t.timeit(number=10000)
```

```python
t = timeit.Timer("factorial_iterative(10)", globals=globals())
time_iterative = t.timeit(number=10000)

print("Average time for recursive:", time_recursive / 10000,
"seconds")
print("Average time for iterative:", time_iterative / 10000,
"seconds")
```

In this example, we compare the average execution times of the factorial_recursive and factorial_iterative functions.

Profiling with cProfile

The cProfile module provides a deterministic profiler that records the time spent in each function call in a program. It helps identify which functions consume the most time, allowing developers to focus on optimizing critical parts of the code.

Running cProfile from the Command Line

To profile a Python script using cProfile from the command line, you can use the following command:

- *Bash:*

```
python -m cProfile script.py
```

The output will display the number of calls, total time, and time per call for each function in the script.

Running cProfile Programmatically

You can also use cProfile programmatically in your Python code.

- **Python:**

```python
import cProfile

def fibonacci_recursive(n):
    if n <= 1:
        return n
    return fibonacci_recursive(n - 1) + fibonacci_recursive(n - 2)

cProfile.run("fibonacci_recursive(30)")
```

The output will display the profiling information for the fibonacci_recursive function.

Analyzing cProfile Results with pstats

The pstats module allows you to interactively analyze the profiling results generated by cProfile. You can sort and display the profiling data to find performance bottlenecks.

- ***Python:***

```python
import cProfile
import pstats

def fibonacci_recursive(n):
    if n <= 1:
        return n
    return fibonacci_recursive(n - 1) + fibonacci_recursive(n - 2)

cProfile.run("fibonacci_recursive(30)", "profile_stats")
p = pstats.Stats("profile_stats")
p.sort_stats("time").print_stats()
```

In this example, we save the profiling results to a file named "profile_stats" and then use pstats to sort and display the results sorted by the time spent in each function call.

Optimization Techniques

After profiling your code and identifying performance bottlenecks, you can apply various optimization techniques to improve its efficiency. Some common optimization techniques include:

- Memoization: Caching intermediate results to avoid redundant computations.

- Algorithm Optimization: Identifying and implementing more efficient algorithms for specific tasks.
- Avoiding Unnecessary Computation: Eliminating unnecessary loops or calculations.
- Using Built-in Functions: Leveraging built-in Python functions and libraries for optimized operations.

Profiling and optimizing code are essential steps in software development to ensure that programs run efficiently and meet performance requirements. Python provides built-in modules like timeit and cProfile that help developers profile code execution time and identify performance bottlenecks. By using these tools and applying optimization techniques, developers can improve the performance of their Python code and deliver faster and more efficient applications. Happy profiling and optimizing!

18. Virtual Environments and Package Management:

18.1. CREATING AND MANAGING VIRTUAL ENVIRONMENTS (VENV, CONDA)

18.2. INSTALLING AND MANAGING PACKAGES (PIP)

18.1. CREATING AND MANAGING VIRTUAL ENVIRONMENTS (VENV, CONDA)

Creating and managing virtual environments in Python, using tools like venv and conda, is a crucial aspect of modern Python development. Virtual environments enable developers to isolate their projects' dependencies, ensuring that different projects can have their own set of libraries without conflicts. This practice promotes reproducibility, portability, and simplifies dependency management, making it easier to share code with others.

Introduction to Virtual Environments:

Python, being a popular and versatile programming language, has a vast ecosystem of libraries and packages that developers can utilize in their projects. However, the downside of this abundance is the potential for conflicts between dependencies. Different projects may require different versions of the same library, which can lead to issues like version clashes or unintended behaviour. To address this problem, virtual environments were introduced.

A virtual environment is a self-contained directory that holds a specific Python interpreter and a set of packages installed for a particular project. When activated, the virtual environment becomes the primary Python environment for the project, effectively isolating it from the system-wide Python environment.

Python's Built-in venv:

Python comes with a built-in module called venv, which allows users to create lightweight virtual environments. To create a virtual environment using venv, you can run the following command in your terminal or command prompt:

```
python -m venv myenv
```

This command creates a new directory named myenv, containing a copy of the Python interpreter and standard library. Additionally, it includes a pip executable that can be used to install packages specifically for this virtual environment.

To activate the virtual environment, you use the appropriate command for your operating system:

On Windows:

```
myenv\Scripts\activate
```

On macOS and Linux:

```
source myenv/bin/activate
```

After activation, any packages you install using pip will be placed into the virtual environment, keeping them separate from the global Python environment.

Managing Packages with pip:

Once you have a virtual environment activated, you can install packages as usual using pip. The packages will be installed locally within the virtual environment's directory.

For example, to install the popular library requests in the virtual environment, you would run:

```
pip install requests
```

This ensures that the requests library is only available within the virtual environment and will not interfere with other projects or the system-wide Python installation.

Deactivating and Deleting Virtual Environments:

When you're done working in a virtual environment, you can deactivate it using the deactivate command:

```
deactivate
```

This will return you to the system-wide Python environment.

If you want to delete the virtual environment entirely, simply remove its directory using the appropriate command for your operating system:

On Windows:

```
rmdir /s /q myenv
```

On macOS and Linux:

```
rm -rf myenv
```

Conda: _An Alternative Package Manager and Environment Manager:_

While venv is sufficient for creating simple virtual environments, it is limited when dealing with complex scientific and data-oriented libraries that have compiled dependencies. Conda is an open-source package manager and environment manager that addresses these limitations. It was initially designed to manage packages in the context of data science and scientific computing but has since grown in popularity and is widely used for general Python development.

To create a new conda environment, you use the following command:

```
conda create --name myenv
```

This will create a new environment named myenv that contains a Python interpreter and basic packages. To activate the environment, you use:

```
conda activate myenv
```

Conda allows you to install packages from the Anaconda repository or the wider Python ecosystem using the conda command. For example:

```
conda install numpy
```

You can also use pip within a conda environment to install packages that are not available in the conda repositories:

```
pip install requests
```

Conda's powerful feature is its ability to handle dependencies and resolve package conflicts automatically. It can manage both Python packages and non-Python libraries, making it ideal for scientific computing where projects often have complex dependencies beyond the Python ecosystem.

Conda allows you to manage not only the packages but also the entire environments, including exporting and importing environments across different systems. This makes it easier to replicate the development environment on multiple machines.

To export the environment to a YAML file:

```
conda env export > environment.yml
```

To create an environment from the YAML file on another system:

```
conda env create -f environment.yml
```

This is especially helpful when collaborating with others on a project or deploying it to a different server.

Creating and managing virtual environments in Python, whether using the built-in venv or the powerful conda, is a best practice for modern Python development. It ensures that each project has its isolated environment, preventing dependency conflicts and facilitating reproducibility. Whether you're working on simple scripts or complex scientific applications, leveraging virtual environments helps keep your Python projects organized, maintainable, and portable.

18.2. Installing and Managing Packages (pip)

Installing and managing packages using pip is an essential skill for any Python developer. pip is the default package manager for Python, and it allows you to install, upgrade, and remove Python packages from the Python Package Index (PyPI) or other package repositories. In this explanation, we will cover the basics of using pip to install and manage packages.

Installing Packages with pip:

To install a package using pip, open your terminal or command prompt and run the following command:

```
pip install package_name
```

Replace package_name with the name of the package you want to install. For example, to install the popular library requests, you would run:

```
pip install requests
```

pip will download the package from PyPI and its dependencies, and then install it into your Python environment.

Specifying Package Versions:

By default, pip will install the latest version of a package. However, you can specify a specific version or a version range using the package name followed by the version number:

```
pip install package_name==1.2.3
```

This installs version 1.2.3 of the package. If you want to install any version within a specific range, you can use comparison operators:

```
pip install package_name>=1.2,<2.0
```

This installs any version equal to or greater than 1.2 but less than 2.0.

Upgrading Packages:

To upgrade a package to the latest available version, use the --upgrade or -U flag:

```
pip install --upgrade package_name
```

This will check for updates and install the latest version if available.

Uninstalling Packages:

If you no longer need a package in your Python environment,

you can uninstall it using the uninstall command or its shorthand un:

```
pip uninstall package_name
```

This will remove the specified package and its dependencies from the environment.

Listing Installed Packages:

To see a list of all packages installed in your environment, you can use the list command or its shorthand freeze:

```
pip list
```

This will display a list of installed packages along with their versions.

Requirements Files:

A requirements file is a text file that lists all the required packages for a project, including their specific versions. This file can be shared with others to reproduce the exact environment used in the project. To generate a requirements file, use the freeze command and redirect the output to a file:

```
pip freeze > requirements.txt
```

To install packages from a requirements file, use the install command with the -r flag:

```
pip install -r requirements.txt
```

This will install all the packages and their respective versions listed in the file.

Searching for Packages:

If you're looking for a specific package or want to discover new packages, you can use the search command:

```
pip search package_name
```

This will display a list of packages matching the given name.

pip is an indispensable tool for Python developers, as it simplifies the process of installing and managing packages from PyPI and other repositories. By mastering pip, you can efficiently handle dependencies, keep your projects up-to-date, and create reproducible development environments. As the Python ecosystem continues to grow, pip remains the go-to tool for managing packages and enabling seamless collaboration within the Python community.

19. Python Best Practices:

19.1. Code organization and style (PEP 8)

19.2. Documentation (docstrings)

19.3. Code versioning and collaboration (Git, GitHub)

19.1. Code organization and style (PEP 8)

Code organization and style play a crucial role in the development of Python applications. They refer to the practices and guidelines that developers follow to structure their codebase in a clear, maintainable, and consistent manner. The Python community has established a set of conventions known as PEP 8 (Python Enhancement Proposal 8) to standardize code organization and style, ensuring that code is readable and easily understandable by others.

PEP 8 covers various aspects of code organization and style, including indentation, line length, naming conventions, and more. By adhering to these guidelines, developers can create code that is not only aesthetically pleasing but also encourages collaboration and reduces the likelihood of introducing bugs. Let's delve into the key aspects of code organization and style as defined by PEP 8.

1. Indentation:

Python uses indentation to define block structures, such as loops and conditionals, instead of explicit braces. PEP 8 recommends using four spaces for indentation, which improves code readability and maintains a consistent visual structure.

2. _Line Length:_

To enhance code readability, PEP 8 suggests limiting lines to a maximum of 79 characters. For comments and documentation, the limit is 72 characters. However, this can be extended up to 99 characters if necessary.

3. _Blank Lines:_

Appropriate usage of blank lines improves code organization and readability. PEP 8 recommends using two blank lines to separate top-level functions and classes, and one blank line between methods within a class.

4. _Import Statements:_

Import statements are crucial for including external modules and packages. PEP 8 suggests organizing imports in the following order: standard library modules, third-party modules, and local application-specific modules. Each category should be separated by a blank line.

5. _Naming Conventions:_

Consistent and descriptive naming is essential for code readability. PEP 8 provides conventions for naming variables, functions, classes, and modules. For example, variable and function names should be in lowercase, with words separated by underscores (snake_case), while class names should be in CamelCase.

6. *Whitespace:*

Proper usage of whitespace can significantly improve code readability. PEP 8 recommends avoiding extraneous whitespace, such as trailing whitespace at the end of lines.

7. Comments and Documentation:

Meaningful comments and docstrings (documentation strings) are vital for understanding code functionality. PEP 8 provides guidelines for writing clear and concise comments and docstrings, making it easier for others to comprehend the code's purpose.

8. *Function and Method Arguments:*

When defining functions or methods, PEP 8 suggests using spaces around the "=" sign for default argument values and avoiding spaces around the parentheses containing the arguments.

9. *Line Breaks:*

To maintain readability, PEP 8 advises breaking lines at operators rather than using backslashes for line continuation. Additionally, it is recommended to add extra indentation on continuation lines for better visual distinction.

10. Avoiding Global Variables:

PEP 8 encourages minimizing the use of global variables, as they can lead to code that is difficult to reason about and maintain.

11. Exception Handling:

When handling exceptions, PEP 8 advises using a specific exception class rather than a broad "except" clause. This practice helps in identifying and handling specific error conditions more effectively.

By adhering to PEP 8 guidelines, Python developers can create clean, organized, and maintainable code. Adopting these conventions not only improves collaboration within development teams but also fosters a more significant sense of cohesion within the Python community. Many Python code editors and IDEs also support automatic PEP 8 code formatting, making it easier for developers to follow these conventions consistently.

It is essential to note that while PEP 8 provides valuable recommendations, there may be cases where adhering strictly to the guidelines is not practical or desirable. In such situations, developers should prioritize code readability and maintainability over strict adherence to PEP 8. Nevertheless, following PEP 8 is generally considered a best practice, as it helps ensure that Python code is of high quality and consistent across projects.

Code examples with explanations:

1. Indentation and Line Length:

```python
def print_numbers():
    for i in range(1, 11):
        if i % 2 == 0:
            print(f"Even: {i}")
        else:
            print(f"Odd: {i}")

print_numbers()
```

In this example, we have a function print_numbers() that prints numbers from 1 to 10 and labels them as even or odd. The indentation is consistent with four spaces, and each line is kept within the 79-character limit.

2. Naming Conventions and Whitespace:

```python
class Dog:
    def __init__(self, name, age):
        self.name = name
        self.age = age

    def bark(self):
```

```python
        print(f"{self.name} says: Woof!")

    def fetch_ball(self, ball_color):
        print(f"{self.name} is fetching the {ball_color} ball.")
```

Here, we have a class Dog with methods bark() and
fetch_ball(). The class name follows the CamelCase
convention, and method names use snake_case. Proper
whitespace is used around the "=" sign in the constructor
(__init__).

3. Import Statements:

```python
import os
import sys
import requests

from utils import helper_function

# Rest of the code
```

The import statements follow the recommended PEP 8 order:
first, standard library modules (os and sys), then third-party
modules (requests), and finally local application-specific
modules (helper_function from the utils module).

4. Comments and Documentation:

```python
def add_numbers(a, b):
    """
    This function adds two numbers and returns the result.

    Parameters:
        a (int): The first number.
        b (int): The second number.

    Returns:
        int: The sum of the two numbers.
    """
    return a + b
```

The function add_numbers() has a docstring that explains its purpose, parameters, and return value. Properly documenting functions in this way makes it easier for other developers to understand and use the function correctly.

5. Line Breaks and Continuation:

```python
long_expression_result = (some_long_variable_name +
another_long_variable_name -
          some_other_variable_name * yet_another_long_variable)
```

In this example, a long expression is broken into multiple lines to maintain the line length within the recommended limit. The continuation lines are indented to make the code visually clear.

```python
try:
    result = perform_calculation(dividend, divisor)
except ZeroDivisionError as e:
    print("Error: Cannot divide by zero.")
except ValueError as e:
    print(f"Error: Invalid input - {e}")
else:
    print(f"The result is: {result}")
```

In this code snippet, specific exception classes (ZeroDivisionError and ValueError) are used to catch and handle specific types of exceptions, following the PEP 8 recommendation.

Remember that PEP 8 guidelines are not rigid rules but rather best practices that promote readable and maintainable code. It's essential to adapt and use them as needed while maintaining code clarity and consistency within the project and team.

19.2. Documentation (Docstrings)

Documentation, particularly docstrings, is a crucial aspect of code organization and style in Python. Docstrings are strings used to provide documentation for functions, classes, and modules. They serve as inline documentation, providing information about the purpose, usage, parameters, and return values of the code elements they describe.

PEP 257, titled "Docstring Conventions," provides guidelines for writing docstrings in Python. These guidelines help developers create consistent and informative documentation that can be easily understood by other developers and tools.

Let's explore the key aspects of documentation, including the importance of docstrings and the recommended conventions for writing them.

1. Importance of Docstrings:

- Enhancing Code Readability: Docstrings act as a quick reference for developers trying to understand how to use a function or class. They provide clear explanations of the code's purpose and behavior.

- Supporting Code Maintenance: Well-documented code is easier to maintain because developers can quickly grasp the intent of various code elements.
- Promoting Collaboration: When working in a team, comprehensive docstrings allow team members to collaborate effectively by providing insights into each other's code.
- Facilitating Code Inspection: Automated tools and IDEs can use docstrings to generate documentation or display context-aware help while coding, improving productivity.

2. Writing Docstrings:

- Triple Quotes: Docstrings are usually enclosed within triple quotes (either single or double) to span multiple lines.
- Docstring Location: Docstrings are placed immediately below the function, class, or module definition, and they are the first statement after the definition.
- Format: PEP 257 recommends using a consistent format for docstrings. The docstring should start with a summary line, followed by an empty line, and then a more detailed description.
- Parameters: For functions and methods, docstrings should list the parameters, their types, and a brief description of each parameter's purpose.
- Return Value: For functions that return a value, the docstring should describe the expected return value and its type.

- Examples: Including usage examples in docstrings can provide practical insights into how to use the code element.

```
def calculate_square(number):
    """
    Calculate the square of a given number.

    Parameters:
        number (int): The input number for which the square
will be calculated.

    Returns:
        int: The square of the input number.
    """
    return number ** 2
```

In this example, the docstring provides a concise summary of the function's purpose, describes the parameter, and states the return value.

3. Handling Docstring Exceptions:

- Omitting Docstrings: It is acceptable to omit docstrings for very simple functions that are self-explanatory. However, it is good practice to include docstrings for most functions, especially those used across different modules or by other developers.

- Non-public Functions: Docstrings for non-public functions (functions with names starting with a single underscore) are optional. However, documenting them can still be beneficial, especially when they are part of a public API.

Overall, following the docstring conventions outlined in PEP 257 helps create consistent and informative documentation, leading to better code organization, improved collaboration, and increased code maintainability. By making use of docstrings, Python developers can ensure that their code is well-documented and readily understandable by others, contributing to a more efficient and productive development process.

Additional Points:

1. Docstring Styles:

- There are several docstring styles used in the Python community. The two most common styles are the one-line style and the multi-line style.
- One-Line Style: In this style, the entire docstring fits into a single line. It is suitable for simple functions or methods.

```python
def square(number):
    """Return the square of the input number."""
    return number ** 2
```

- Multi-Line Style: This style includes a multi-line docstring with detailed descriptions for each parameter, return value, and usage examples. It is recommended for more complex functions and classes.

```python
def divide(dividend, divisor):
    """
    Divide the dividend by the divisor and return the result.

    Parameters:
        dividend (int): The number to be divided.
        divisor (int): The number by which the dividend will be
divided.

    Returns:
        float: The result of the division.
    """
    return dividend / divisor
```

2. Handling Exceptional Cases:

- Docstrings should also mention any exceptions or errors that a function or method may raise, providing insights into potential error scenarios.
- For example, if a function raises a custom exception, it is beneficial to document the situations in which that exception might occur.

3. *Docstring Tools and Standards:*

- Several tools and libraries exist to assist with documenting Python code. Popular ones include Sphinx, Doxygen, and Google-style docstrings.
- Google-style docstrings follow a specific convention where the docstring starts with a summary line, followed by more detailed descriptions, parameters, and return values. This style is used by Google and adopted by some open-source projects.

```python
def multiply(a, b):
    """

    Multiply two numbers.

    Args:
        a (int): The first number.
        b (int): The second number.

    Returns:
        int: The product of a and b.
    """

    return a * b
```

4. *Maintaining Updated Documentation:*

- As code evolves and changes, it's essential to keep the docstrings up to date to reflect the current behavior of functions, methods, and classes.

- Whenever there are changes in the behavior or API of a code element, updating the docstrings helps ensure that users are aware of the modifications.

5. *Multi-line Strings and Docstrings:*

- Python allows multi-line strings (strings enclosed within triple quotes) outside of docstrings.
- While multi-line strings can be used for comments and block documentation, they do not serve the same purpose as docstrings. Docstrings are specifically intended for providing inline documentation for code elements.

6. *Using Type Annotations in Docstrings:*

- With the introduction of type annotations in Python 3.5 and later, docstrings can also include information about the expected types of parameters and return values.
- This practice helps provide additional clarity on the data types that the function or method accepts and returns.

7. *Translating Docstrings:*

- In multi-lingual projects, it is common to have docstrings translated into different languages for better internationalization and localization (i18n and l10n).

- Special tools, like Sphinx, support generating documentation in multiple languages by providing translations of docstrings.

Following these additional points and guidelines ensures that your Python code is well-documented, making it more accessible to other developers and promoting good coding practices throughout your projects. Well-documented code not only aids in understanding your codebase but also contributes to the overall success of your software development endeavors.

19.3. Code versioning and collaboration (Git, GitHub)

Code versioning and collaboration are essential aspects of modern software development. They involve using version control systems like Git and platforms like GitHub to manage and track changes to code, facilitate teamwork, and ensure the development process remains efficient and organized. Let's delve into the significance of code versioning and collaboration using Git and GitHub.

1. Code Versioning with Git:

- Git is a distributed version control system widely used in the software development community.
- Version control allows developers to track changes to their code over time, enabling them to revert to previous versions, view differences between versions, and collaborate seamlessly with others.
- With Git, each developer has their own local repository, and changes are committed and tracked locally before being pushed to a central repository or a remote service like GitHub.

2. *Benefits of Code Versioning:*

- History Tracking: Git maintains a complete history of code changes, allowing developers to understand who made a change, when, and why.
- Branching and Merging: Git enables developers to create branches to work on features or bug fixes independently, and then merge the changes back into the main codebase once they are ready.
- Collaboration: Git facilitates collaboration among team members, preventing conflicts and providing mechanisms for resolving them when they occur.
- Code Backup: By using Git, developers ensure that their codebase is securely backed up, reducing the risk of data loss.

3. *GitHub for Collaboration:*

- GitHub is a popular web-based hosting service for Git repositories. It provides a platform for developers to share and collaborate on code.
- Developers can push their local Git repositories to GitHub, making it accessible to others and enabling seamless collaboration.
- GitHub offers features like pull requests, issue tracking, code reviews, and project management tools, which streamline the development workflow.

4. Pull Requests and Code Review:

- Pull requests are GitHub's mechanism for proposing changes from one branch to another, typically from a feature branch to the main branch (e.g., from "feature" to "master").
- Code review is a crucial part of the pull request process, where team members review the proposed changes, provide feedback, and ensure code quality before merging.

5. Issue Tracking and Project Management:

- GitHub's issue tracking system allows developers to report bugs, request new features, or discuss improvements for a project.
- Issues can be assigned to specific team members, tagged with labels, and tracked throughout their lifecycle.
- GitHub's project management tools, such as boards and milestones, help teams organize tasks and keep track of progress during development.

6. Continuous Integration (CI) and Continuous Deployment (CD):

- GitHub integrates with various CI/CD services, enabling developers to automate testing, building, and deployment processes.

- Continuous Integration ensures that changes are regularly integrated into the main codebase, promoting a stable and reliable development environment.
- Continuous Deployment automates the release process, allowing teams to deliver code changes to production rapidly and efficiently.

7. Community and Open Source:

- GitHub hosts a vast open-source community, where developers can collaborate on projects, contribute to existing repositories, and gain recognition for their work.
- Open-source projects on GitHub often invite contributions from the community through pull requests, fostering a collaborative and inclusive development culture.

In conclusion, code versioning with Git and collaboration on platforms like GitHub are critical for modern software development practices. By utilizing these tools, developers can efficiently manage their codebase, collaborate seamlessly, and ensure a smooth and productive development workflow. These practices not only enhance code quality and reliability but also foster a vibrant and thriving open-source community.

Appendix: [[370]]

- **EXERCISES AND SOLUTIONS [[371]]**
- **RESOURCES**

Exercises and Solutions:

Exercises:

1. Fibonacci Sequence:

Write a Python function to generate the Fibonacci sequence up to a given number 'n'. The Fibonacci sequence starts with 0 and 1, and each subsequent number is the sum of the two preceding ones. For example, if 'n' is 10, the function should return [0, 1, 1, 2, 3, 5, 8].

2. Prime Number Checker:

Create a Python function that takes an integer as input and returns True if the number is prime and False otherwise. A prime number is a natural number greater than 1 that has no positive divisors other than 1 and itself. For example, if the input is 17, the function should return True.

3. Palindrome Check:

Write a Python function that checks if a given string is a palindrome. A palindrome is a word, phrase, number, or other sequence that reads the same backward as forward. For example, if the input is "radar," the function should return True.

4. Reverse Words in a Sentence:

Write a Python function that takes a sentence as input and returns the sentence with the order of words reversed. For example, if the input is "Python is awesome," the function should return "awesome is Python."

5. List Comprehension:

Create a Python function that takes a list of integers as input and returns a new list containing only the even numbers using list comprehension.

6. Factorial Calculation:

Write a Python function to calculate the factorial of a given positive integer 'n'. The factorial of a non-negative integer 'n' is the product of all positive integers less than or equal to 'n'. For example, if 'n' is 5, the function should return 120 (1 * 2 * 3 * 4 * 5).

7. Anagram Checker:

Create a Python function that takes two strings as input and returns True if the two strings are anagrams of each other and False otherwise. Anagrams are words or phrases formed by rearranging the letters of another word or phrase, typically using all the original letters exactly once. For example, if the inputs are "listen" and "silent," the function should return True.

8. File Word Counter:

Write a Python function that takes the name of a text file as input and returns the total number of words in the file.

9. Matrix Transpose:

Create a Python function that takes a matrix (2D list) as input and returns the transpose of the matrix. The transpose of a matrix is obtained by swapping its rows and columns. For example, if the input is [[1, 2, 3], [4, 5, 6]], the function should return [[1, 4], [2, 5], [3, 6]].

10. Random Password Generator:

Write a Python function that generates a random password of a given length 'n'. The password should consist of a mix of uppercase letters, lowercase letters, and digits.

11. Recursive Sum:

Create a Python function that takes a list of integers as input and returns the sum of all the elements in the list using recursion.

12. Roman Numeral Converter:

Write a Python function that converts a given integer to its Roman numeral representation. Roman numerals are represented by combinations of letters from the set {I, V, X, L, C, D, M}. For example, if the input is 2023, the function should return "MMXXIII."

13. Longest Common Prefix:

Create a Python function that takes a list of strings as input and returns the longest common prefix among all the strings. For example, if the input is ["apple", "apricot", "aptitude"], the function should return "ap".

14. Count Character Occurrences:

Create a Python function that takes a string and a character as input and returns the number of times the character appears in the string.

15. Find Largest Element in a List:

Write a Python function that takes a list of numbers as input and returns the largest element in the list.

16. Remove Duplicates from a List:

Create a Python function that takes a list as input and returns
a new list with duplicates removed while preserving the
original order of elements.

17. Unique Characters in a String:

Write a Python function that takes a string as input and
returns True if all the characters in the string are unique, and
False if there are any repeated characters.

18. Binary Search:

Implement a Python function that performs a binary search
on a sorted list of integers. The function should return the
index of the target element if found, or -1 if the element is
not present in the list.

19. Time Conversion:

Write a Python function that takes a time in 12-hour format
(e.g., "03:45 PM") as input and returns the time in 24-hour
format (e.g., "15:45").

20. Dictionary Merge:

Create a Python function that takes two dictionaries as input
and returns a new dictionary that is a result of merging both
dictionaries.

Solutions:

1. Fibonacci Sequence:

```python
def generate_fibonacci_sequence(n):
    sequence = [0, 1]
    while sequence[-1] + sequence[-2] <= n:
        next_number = sequence[-1] + sequence[-2]
        sequence.append(next_number)
    return sequence

# Test the function
n = 10
print(generate_fibonacci_sequence(n))  # Output: [0, 1, 1, 2, 3, 5, 8]
```

2. Prime Number Checker:

```python
def is_prime(number):
    if number <= 1:
        return False
    for i in range(2, int(number**0.5) + 1):
        if number % i == 0:
            return False
    return True

# Test the function
num = 17
print(is_prime(num))  # Output: True
```

3. Palindrome Check:

```python
def is_palindrome(word):
    return word == word[::-1]
```

```python
# Test the function
string = "radar"
print(is_palindrome(string))  # Output: True
```

4. *Reverse Words in a Sentence:*

```python
def reverse_words(sentence):
    words = sentence.split()
    reversed_sentence = " ".join(reversed(words))
    return reversed_sentence

# Test the function
sentence = "Python is awesome"
print(reverse_words(sentence))  # Output: "awesome is Python"
```

5. *List Comprehension:*

```python
def get_even_numbers(numbers):
    return [num for num in numbers if num % 2 == 0]

# Test the function
numbers_list = [1, 2, 3, 4, 5, 6, 7, 8, 9, 10]
print(get_even_numbers(numbers_list))  # Output: [2, 4, 6, 8, 10]
```

6. *Factorial Calculation:*

```python
def factorial(n):
    if n == 0:
        return 1
    else:
        return n * factorial(n - 1)

# Test the function
```

```python
num = 5
print(factorial(num))  # Output: 120
```

7. Anagram Checker:

```python
def are_anagrams(str1, str2):
    return sorted(str1) == sorted(str2)


# Test the function
word1 = "listen"
word2 = "silent"
print(are_anagrams(word1, word2))  # Output: True
```

8. File Word Counter:

```python
def count_words_in_file(file_name):
    with open(file_name, 'r') as file:
        content = file.read()
        word_list = content.split()
        return len(word_list)


# Test the function
file_name = "example.txt"
print(count_words_in_file(file_name))
```

9. Matrix Transpose:

```python
def transpose_matrix(matrix):
    return [list(row) for row in zip(*matrix)]


# Test the function
matrix = [[1, 2, 3], [4, 5, 6]]
print(transpose_matrix(matrix))  # Output: [[1, 4], [2, 5], [3, 6]]
```

10. Random Password Generator:

```python
import random
import string

def generate_random_password(length):
    characters = string.ascii_letters + string.digits
    password = ''.join(random.choice(characters) for _ in
range(length))
    return password

# Test the function
length = 10
print(generate_random_password(length))
```

11. Recursive Sum:

```python
def recursive_sum(numbers):
    if len(numbers) == 0:
        return 0
    else:
        return numbers[0] + recursive_sum(numbers[1:])

# Test the function
numbers_list = [1, 2, 3, 4, 5]
print(recursive_sum(numbers_list))  # Output: 15
```

12. Roman Numeral Converter:

```python
def int_to_roman(number):
    val = [
        1000, 900, 500, 400,
        100, 90, 50, 40,
        10, 9, 5, 4,
        1
```

```python
    ]
    syms = [
        "M", "CM", "D", "CD",
        "C", "XC", "L", "XL",
        "X", "IX", "V", "IV",
        "I"
    ]
    roman_numeral = ""
    i = 0
    while number > 0:
        for _ in range(number // val[i]):
            roman_numeral += syms[i]
            number -= val[i]
        i += 1
    return roman_numeral


# Test the function
num = 2023
print(int_to_roman(num))  # Output: "MMXXIII"
```

13. *Longest Common Prefix:*

```python
def longest_common_prefix(strings):
    if not strings:
        return ""
    prefix = strings[0]
    for string in strings[1:]:
        i = 0
        while i < len(prefix) and i < len(string) and prefix[i] == string[i]:
            i += 1
        prefix = prefix[:i]
    return prefix


# Test the function
words_list = ["apple", "apricot", "aptitude"]
```

```python
print(longest_common_prefix(words_list))
```

14. Count Character Occurrences:

```python
def count_occurrences(text, char):
    return text.count(char)

# Test the function
text = "python programming"
character = "m"
print(count_occurrences(text, character))  # Output: 2
```

15. Find Largest Element in a List:

```python
def find_largest_element(numbers):
    return max(numbers)

# Test the function
numbers_list = [4, 9, 2, 7, 5]
print(find_largest_element(numbers_list))  # Output: 9
```

16. Remove Duplicates from a List:

```python
def remove_duplicates(input_list):
    return list(dict.fromkeys(input_list))

# Test the function
original_list = [1, 2, 2, 3, 4, 4, 5]
print(remove_duplicates(original_list))  # Output: [1, 2, 3, 4, 5]
```

17. Unique Characters in a String:

```python
def has_unique_characters(input_string):
    return len(set(input_string)) == len(input_string)
```

```python
# Test the function
word = "banana"
print(has_unique_characters(word))  # Output: False
```

18. *Binary Search:*

```python
def binary_search(sorted_list, target):
    low, high = 0, len(sorted_list) - 1
    while low <= high:
        mid = (low + high) // 2
        if sorted_list[mid] == target:
            return mid
        elif sorted_list[mid] < target:
            low = mid + 1
        else:
            high = mid - 1
    return -1

# Test the function
sorted_numbers = [1, 2, 3, 4, 5, 6, 7, 8, 9]
target_number = 5
print(binary_search(sorted_numbers, target_number))  # Output: 4
```

19. *Time Conversion:*

```python
def time_conversion(time_string):
    hours, minutes = time_string.split(":")
    am_pm = time_string[-2:]
    if am_pm == "PM" and hours != "12":
        hours = str(int(hours) + 12)
    elif am_pm == "AM" and hours == "12":
        hours = "00"
    return f"{hours}:{minutes}"
```

```python
# Test the function
time_12h = "03:45 PM"
print(time_conversion(time_12h))  # Output: "15:45"
```

20. Dictionary Merge:

```python
def merge_dictionaries(dict1, dict2):
    merged_dict = dict1.copy()
    merged_dict.update(dict2)
    return merged_dict

# Test the function
dict1 = {"a": 1, "b": 2}
dict2 = {"c": 3, "d": 4}
print(merge_dictionaries(dict1, dict2))

# Output: {'a': 1, 'b': 2, 'c': 3, 'd': 4}
```

Feel free to use these exercises and solutions to test your understanding and enhance your Python skills. Happy coding!

RESOURCES:

1. NSWorldInfo

Website: https://nsworldinfo.medium.com/

- Python Mastery Series:
  https://nsworldinfo.medium.com/list/python-mastery-complete-python-series-from-novice-to-pro-59845ee05372
- Data Science List:
  https://nsworldinfo.medium.com/list/data-science-29618c7ebc31

2. Tech NS Arena

YouTube Channel: https://youtube.com/@TechNSArena

This channel provides informative insights on Data Science, Machine Learning, Python Programming, Technology, and related fields through engaging video content.

3. InfoWorldwithNS

Blog: https://infoworldwithns.blogspot.com/

This blog offers informative insights on Data Science, Machine Learning, Python Programming, Artificial Intelligence, Technology, and related fields. It includes real-world code snippets with easy-to-understand explanations, making it a valuable resource for learners.

4. Tech NS Oracle

Page: https://bmc.link/technsoracle

Tech NS Oracle provides informative insights on Data Science, Machine Learning, Python Programming, Artificial Intelligence, Technology, and related fields. Explore this page for enriching content and stay updated with the latest trends and developments in the tech world.

These additional resources complement "Python Mastery: From Absolute Beginner to Pro" by offering readers the opportunity to explore more in-depth topics, engage with multimedia content, and access real-world examples. Whether you prefer written articles or engaging video content, these resources are sure to further enhance your Python journey and deepen your understanding of the fascinating world of technology.

End-Description:

Congratulations on completing your transformative journey through "Python Mastery: From Absolute Beginner to Pro"! This comprehensive and engaging book has been meticulously crafted to empower aspiring programmers like you, equipping you with the knowledge and skills to unlock the full potential of Python.

From the very beginning, you delved into the fundamentals of Python, learning about data types, variables, and control structures. As you progressed, you gained confidence, and the mysteries of functions, modules, and object-oriented programming became clear. Real-world projects provided you with hands-on experience, and you built applications that showcased the practical applications of Python.

In the advanced sections, you embraced more complex concepts, such as file handling, database interactions, and web development using frameworks like Flask and Django. Exploring machine learning and data science with Python opened up exciting opportunities for analyzing and visualizing data, making predictions, and solving real-world problems.

Throughout this book, the focus has been on understanding, not just memorization. You've learned to think like a Python expert, approaching challenges with creativity and problem-solving skills. You are now equipped to tackle coding challenges, design scalable applications, and collaborate on ambitious projects. As you reach the final chapter, you've become part of the vibrant Python community, where your knowledge and passion can inspire and support others on their coding journeys. The possibilities for you, as a Python programmer, are boundless.

Remember, this book is not just an endpoint but a stepping stone to a lifelong journey of continuous learning and growth. Embrace the joy of discovery and the satisfaction of creating something meaningful with your Python skills.

As the author of this book, I want to extend my heartfelt appreciation to you, dear reader. Your dedication and enthusiasm have made this journey even more rewarding. I hope you find the knowledge gained within these pages not only valuable but also empowering.

Thank you for choosing "Python Mastery: From Absolute Beginner to Pro." May your passion for Python continue to fuel your curiosity and drive, leading you to achieve even greater heights in the world of programming and technology.

Happy coding!

Python Mastery: From Absolute Beginner to Pro

NIBEDITA SAHU